SNOW
TRAILS

**Cross-country Ski
and Snowshoe in
Central and Western
New York**

by Rich & Sue Freeman

SNOW
TRAILS

Cross-country Ski and Snowshoe in Central and Western New York

Foot print Press

PO Box 645, Fishers, NY 14453
http://www.footprintpress.com

Other books available from Footprint Press:

Take A Hike! Family Walks in the Rochester (NY) Area
Take A Hike! Family Walks in the Finger Lakes
   & Genesee Valley Region (NY)
Take Your Bike! Family Rides in the Rochester (NY) Area
Take Your Bike! Family Rides in the Finger Lakes
   & Genesee Valley Region (NY)
Bruce Trail – An Adventure Along the Niagara Escarpment
Peak Experiences – Hiking the Highest Summits of New York,
   County by County
Backpacking Trails of Central & Western New York (booklet)
Alter – A Simple Path to Emotional Wellness

Locations by Trail Number

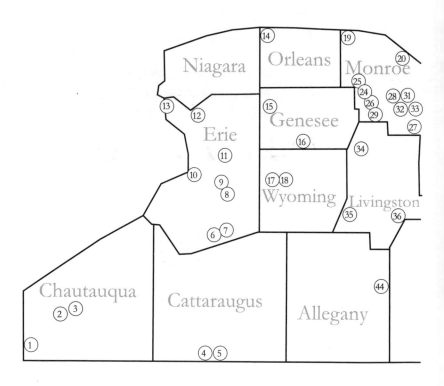

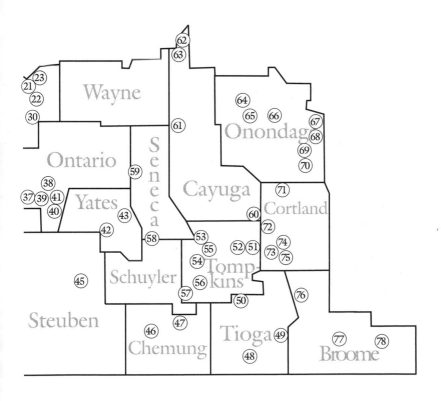

Contents

Acknowledgments

The research, writing, production, and promotion of a book such as this is never a solitary adventure. *Snow Trails* came into being because of the assistance of many wonderful people who freely shared their knowledge, experience, resources, thoughts, and time. We extend our heartfelt thanks to them all. Each in his or her own way is responsible for making central and western New York a better place to live and, most of all, a region rich with the spirit of collaboration for the betterment of all. This is what ensures quality of life. Thank you, each and every one.

Ron Abbott, Pratt's Falls, Onondaga County Parks
Michael Allen, DEC Avon
Melissa Anderson, Cumming Nature Center
Don Baird, Adirondack Mountain Club
David & Liz Beebe, Erie Canal Park
Howard Beye, Finger Lakes Trail Conference
Kevin Brazill, Green Lakes State Park
Dan Carroll, DEC Avon
Allen Coletta, Rochester City Parks Department
Mike Collins, Sprague Brook Park, Erie County Parks
Steve Davison, DEC Cortland
Mark Dominie, Greek Peak Nordic Ski Center
Claire Dunn, SUNY College of Environmental Science & Forestry
James Eckler, DEC Avon
Bob Ellis, Onondaga County Parks
Jim Farr, Rochester City Parks Department
Becky Faulkner, Peek'n Peak Ski Resort
David Forness, DEC Cortland
Bruce Fullem, Sampson State Park
George Fraley, volunteer extraordinaire
Dorothy Gerhart, Iroquois National Wildlife Refuge
John Goodfellow, Four Seasons Ski Center
Fran Gotscik, Genesee Valley Greenway
Brian Grassia, Erie County Forest
Dale Grinolds Jr., Onondaga County Parks
Sally Guydosh, Waterman Conservation Education Center
Bill Harris, Chautauqua County Parks
Ed Hart, Broome County Parks
Rob Hiltbrand, Fair Haven State Park
Eric Johnson, Monroe County Parks
Jerry Jones, Chemung County Parks
John Kalinski, Como Lake Park, Erie County Parks
Mark Keister, DEC Bath
Mike Kelley, Long Point State Park
Eileen Kennedy, Mendon Ponds Park
John Livingston, Green Lakes State Park
Mike Lukas, Emery Park, Erie County Parks
Scott MacDonald, Waterman Conservation Education Center
Theodore Markham, Village of Bath

Charles Marsh, Keuka Lake State Park
Scott Meidenbauer, Bryncliff Resort
Dave Mele, Highland Forest, Onondaga County Parks
Bill Michalek, Beaver Meadow Nature Center
Claudia Minotti, Tanglewood Nature Center
Benjamin Morey, Buckhorn Island State Park
Kevin Moss, Genesee Country Nature Center
Chris Nielsen, Harriet Hollister Spencer Memorial State Recreation Area
Fred Noteboom, South Hill Recreation Way
James Ochterski, Tanglewood Nature Center
Paul Osborn, Genesee County Park
Richard Parker, Letchworth State Park
Don Root, City of Rochester, Water & Lighting Bureau
Tom Rowland, Lakeside Beach State Park
Don Schaufler, Cornell University Department of Natural Resources
Richard Schoch, South Hill Recreation Way
Ron Schroder, DEC Avon
James Schug, Dryden Lake Park
Chuck Schweikert, Erie County Forest
Forest Skelton, Monroe County Parks
Jim Slusarczyk, Hamlin Beach State Park
Linda Spielman, Cayuga Nature Center
Bruce Stebbins, Beaver Lake Nature Center
Wesley Stiles, DEC Cortland
Susannah Touchet, Lime Hollow Nature Center
Martha Twarkins, Finger Lakes National Forest
Marjorie Tweedale, Finger Lakes National Forest
Mark Varvayanis, Dryden Lake Park
Brian Vattimo, Harriet Hollister Spencer Memorial State Recreation Area
Ron Walker, Tinker Nature Park
Karen Wallace, Tifft Nature Preserve
John Weeks, Sterling Park
Meme Yanetsko, Greater Olean, Inc.
James Zimpfer, Harriet Hollister Spencer Memorial State Recreation Area
David Zlomek, DEC Belmont

These people directed us to choice trails, reviewed our maps and descriptions, supplied historical tidbits, and often are responsible for the existence and maintenance of the trails. They have our sincere appreciation.

Introduction

We aren't skiing fanatics. We don't know anything about the latest in boot, ski, or snowshoe technology. We're not well versed on the fine points of technique. But when the snow flies in western New York and our world turns white, we find it hard to stay indoors.

That's the beauty of cross-country skiing and snowshoeing. You don't have to have any special expertise, expensive equipment, or a hardened body to enjoy the sports. All they require are the interest and will to get out and try it. So, for those of you who want to enjoy our winters, we provide this guide—packed with details on where to go for a quick evening outing near home or a longer adventure farther afield. And for you veterans of the white trails—lots of variety.

We've learned that it's hard to plan a ski or snowshoe outing in central and western New York. The snow doesn't always cooperate. It's best to act with spontaneity and head out when the snow flies. As an alternative, check the index in the back listing high elevation trails which get snow earlier and hold it longer than other area trails.

There's another index for areas with ski and/or snowshoe rentals so you can try the sport before investing in equipment.

Most trails listed in this book are free and open to the public. A few require a small admission fee or request a donation. They are clearly noted in the heading to each trail beside the term "Admission." You do not have to be a member of the sponsoring group to enjoy any of the trails.

We have clustered the trails geographically by county. An overall map showing the locations of all the trails can be found on pages 4 and 5.

The indexes at the back list trails by a variety of criteria. Check them out to quickly zero in on trails that suit your purposes.

Sketch maps are provided for each trail. Some trails were never mapped prior to this book. On most of the maps, you'll find a small inset map. This gives a broader picture and lets you visually locate the trail relative to major towns and roads.

Enjoy exploring the trails of central and western New York.

Legend

At the beginning of each trail listing, you will find a description with the following information:

Location: The town and county where the trail is located.

Directions: How to find the trailhead parking area from a major road or town.

Length: How many miles of trails and unplowed roads are available for winter use.

Difficulty: Novice—flat, wide, easy trails, often posted with the Easiest ski symbol:

Intermediate—narrower or steeper trails requiring knowledge of how to control your skis, often posted with the More Difficult ski symbol:

Advanced—steep, narrow trails requiring good control of skis, often posted with the Most Difficult ski symbol:

Terrain: An indication of the aerobic workout you can expect - ranging from flat (little exertion required) to steep hills (maximum exertion required).

Trail Markings: Markings used to designate the trails in this book vary widely. Some trails are not marked at all but can be easily followed. Other trails are well marked with either signs, blazes, or markers, and sometimes a combination of all three. Blazing is done by the official group that maintains the trail.

Signs – wooden or metal signs with instructions in words or pictures.

Blazes – painted markings on trees showing where the trail goes. Many blazes are rectangular and placed at eye level. Colors may be used to denote different trails. If a tree has twin blazes beside one another, you should proceed cautiously because the trail either turns or another trail intersects.

Sometimes you'll see a section of trees with painted markings which aren't neat geometric shapes. These are probably boundary markers or trees marked for logging. Trail blazes are generally distinct geometric shapes and are placed at eye level.

Markers – small plastic or metal geometric shapes (square, round, triangular) nailed to trees at eye level to show where the trail goes. They also may be colored to denote different trails.

It is likely that at some point you will lose the blazes or markers while following a trail. The first thing to do is stop and look around. See if you can spot a blaze or marker by looking in all directions, including behind you. If not, backtrack until you see a blaze or marker, then proceed forward again, carefully following the markings.

Uses: The activity or activities allowed on the trail. Winter activities include skiing, snowshoeing, and snowmobiling. Hiking, is listed if allowed on this trail during non-snow seasons.

Amenities: The services or amenities you'll find at this trail. They include groomed trails, shelter, warming hut, restrooms or outhouses, ski or snowshoe rental, snack bar or restaurant, and anything else unique to the area.

Admission: The entrance fee to use the trails.

Dogs: If dogs are allowed on the trails.

Hours: Time period during which trail use is allowed.

Contact: The address and phone number of the organization to contact if you would like additional information or if you have questions not answered in this book.

For Snow Conditions Call: A phone number or web site where current snow conditions are made available for this trail.

Map Legend

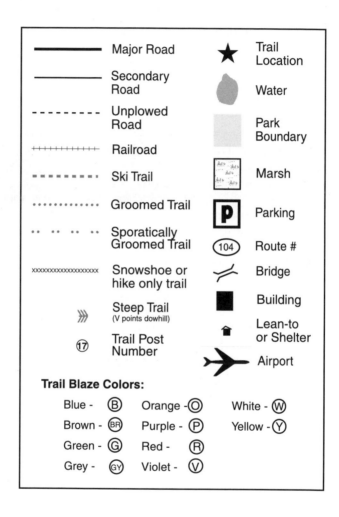

———— Major Road	★ Trail Location
———— Secondary Road	Water
- - - - - - Unplowed Road	Park Boundary
++++++++++ Railroad	Marsh
■ ■ ■ ■ ■ ■ Ski Trail	**P** Parking
•••••••••••• Groomed Trail	(104) Route #
•• •• •• •• Sporatically Groomed Trail	Bridge
xxxxxxxxxxxxxx Snowshoe or hike only trail	■ Building
⟫ Steep Trail (V points dowhill)	Lean-to or Shelter
⑰ Trail Post Number	✈ Airport

Trail Blaze Colors:

Blue - Ⓑ	Orange - Ⓞ	White - Ⓦ
Brown - ⒝ⓡ	Purple - Ⓟ	Yellow - Ⓨ
Green - Ⓖ	Red - Ⓡ	
Grey - ⒢ⓨ	Violet - Ⓥ	

Winter Trail Etiquette

Ski touring and snowshoeing, like any other sports, are much more enjoyable for everyone if all participants follow a few basic rules of etiquette:

Stay on the trails:
Trails are laid out for skiers safety and convenience. Leaving the trail may cause skiers to encounter unknown terrain hazards and become lost.

Pass on a flat area:
Try to pass other skiers on the flat. A faster skier should vocally indicate his or her desire to pass. The slower skier should yield by stepping out of the track to the right where possible. Try not to pass on a downhill. Wait for a flat area where the slower skier can maneuver more easily.

Meeting on a hill:
The skier going downhill has the right of way since he or she is moving faster and may have less control. Do not descend a hill until the trail is clear.

Ski in the correct direction:
Some trails are one-way (identified by arrows on the map). Please ski in the proper direction. If a trail has two sets of tracks, ski the set of tracks on the right side.

Obstructing the trail:
Move off the trail as quickly as possible after a fall. This will prevent possible collisions and allow other skiers to pass. Fill sitzmarks before proceeding.

Don't ski or snowshoe alone:
Long tours, especially should not be attempted alone. Hypothermia is a very real and serious hazard in cold weather and other serious injuries can occur. It would be wise to have a partner available to help if an injury does occur.

Fill in sitzmarks:
A hole in a downhill track can be hazardous to other skiers. Once these freeze they are difficult to fill in.

Do not walk or snowshoe in tracks:
This ruins skiing for everyone. Walk or snowshoe to the side of the trail.

Leave dogs at home:
Dogs leave paw marks and feces on the trail which ruin a good track. They also can be hazardous by getting in the way of skiers and chasing wildlife.

Do not litter:
Carry out what you carry in.

Preparations and Safety

You can enhance your time in the outdoors by dressing properly and carrying appropriate equipment. Even for a short outing, take a small backpack or fanny pack with the following gear:

camera	flashlight
compass	water bottle with water
rain gear	a map (such as this book)
snacks	plastic bag to pick up litter
emergency matches	whistle

In winter, it's important to dress in layers. As you ski or snowshoe, the exertion will generate body heat. Peel off layers so you don't get sweaty. When you stop, put the layers back on to retain heat. You'll need extra space in your day pack to hold the bulky winter layers as you take them off.

Clothing selection is more important in winter than other times of year. If possible, avoid wearing cotton such as blue jeans and T-shirts. Once cotton gets wet it stays wet and increases the body's loss of heat. Select clothing made of wool which retains its heat retention properties even when wet, or synthetics which dry quickly. The synthetics have many names such as nylon, fleece, polypropylene, polyester, Gore-tex®, Duofold®, Capilene®, CoolMax®, and Power Dry®.

The most important layer is your head. Putting a hat on and off is an easy and effective way to control body temperature as your exertion fluctuates.

Skiing or snowshoeing with children is good exercise as well as an opportunity for learning. Use the time to teach children how to read a compass or identify animal tracks. You'll find books on these subjects in the public library.

Make it fun by taking a different type of gorp for each outing. Gorp is any combination of dried foods that you eat as a snack. Examples are:
1) peanuts, M&M's®, and raisins
2) chocolate morsels, nuts, and granola
3) dried banana chips, sunflower seeds, and carob chips

Get creative and mix any combination of chocolate, carob, dried fruits, nuts, oats, granolas, etc. The bulk food section at your local grocery store is a wealth of ideas. Other fun snacks are marshmallows, popcorn, peanuts in shells, graham crackers, and beef jerky.

When on an adventure with a child, tie a string on a whistle and have your child wear it as a necklace for safety. Instruct your child to blow the whistle only if he or she is lost.

A Word on Dogs

Dogs are controversial on trails any time of year, but especially in winter. Yes, they need exercise in winter just like we do, but you need to show good judgement in when and where to take a dog on a winter adventure. In the data listing we have included information on whether dogs are permitted or not on each specific trail. Even where dogs are permitted, please follow these guidelines:

• keep dogs away from groomed trails

• select lesser used trails

• keep the dog under control or on leash at all times

Maps

This book is loaded with sketch maps to give you an idea of where to find each trail network and how to navigate once you get there. We've found the *New York State Atlas & Gazetteer* by DeLorme to be a valuable asset when trying to find a trailhead in unknown territory.

On the trail it's sometimes best to have a topographical map with you. You can order topographical maps from the United States Geological Survey or pick them up at area outdoor stores, generally for $4 apiece. Another option is to visit http://www.topozone.com on the internet to print a topo map of the the area you plan to cover.

Snow Conditions

There's an item in each trail data listing called "For Snow Conditions Call:" This is where we list a phone number to call or web site to visit for the latest update on snow conditions.

For Ithaca area trails, you're invited to join the XCSKI list serve. This is an e-mail list where members report and read about snow conditions in the Ithaca area. To join, send an e-mail message to listproc@cornell.edu. The body of the message should read "subscribe XCSKI-L@cornell.edu. yourID@youraddress yourname." Substitute your e-mail address for yourID@youraddress and your name for yourname.

For updates on Rochester area trail conditions, join the Rochester Nordic Ski Club list serve. To subscribe send an email message to: majordomo@clss.com with the body: subscribe RNSC me@mydomain.com. Substitute your own e-mail address for "me@mydomain.com." Send your skiing tips to the whole group by sending a message to RNSC@clss.com.

Nordic Ski Clubs

Ski clubs are the place to find like-minded people—those who celebrate, not hibernate when the snow flies. Through these organizations you can find camaraderie, assistance, lessons, and challenges.

Binghampton
Triple Cities Ski Club
PO Box 23, Endicott, NY 13760
www.tier.net/tcsc
hotline (607) 723-TCSC

Buffalo
Lederhosen Ski Club
PO Box 326, Amherst, NY 14226
(716) 688-9178

Bell Ski Club
c/o Andy Gierson
777 Blair Valley Road, Youngstown, NY 14174

Ithaca
Cayuga Nordic Ski Club
400 Bean Hill Road, Freeville, NY 13067
www.spidergraphics.com/cnsc/

Rochester
Huggers Ski Club (singles)
PO Box 23921, Rochester, NY 14692
http://huggersskiclub.tripod.com
hotline (716) 865-7910

Rochester Nordic Ski Club
PO Box 22897, Rochester, NY 14692
www.ggw.org/NordicSki
hotline (716) 234-5808

Monroe Y Ski Club (for adults)
YMCA
797 Monroe Avenue, Rochester, NY 14607
www.monroeyskiclub.org

Syracuse
Onondaga Ski Club
PO Box 8025, Teall Station, Syracuse. NY 13217
www.osc-ski.org/home.html
info@osc-ski.org
(315) 422-9382

Chautauqua
&
Cattaraugus
Counties

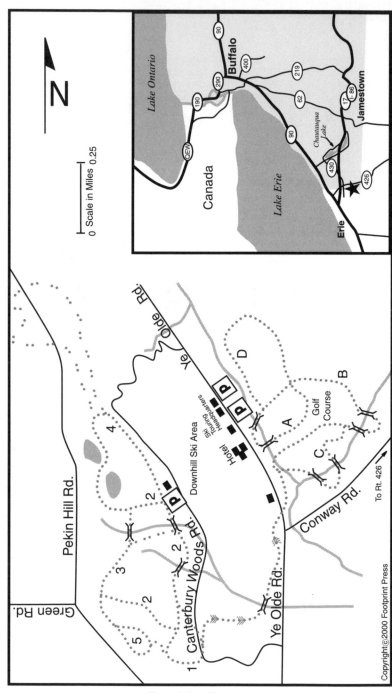

Peek'n Peak

1.

Peek'n Peak

Location:	Clymer, Chautauqua County
Directions:	From Route 17 (now I-86) exit at Findley Lake (Route 426). Take Route 426 south and follow the signs to Peek'n Peak.
Length:	8.6 miles of trails
Difficulty:	Novice, Intermediate
Terrain:	Flat and hilly sections
Trail Markings:	None
Uses:	Skiing
Amenities:	Warming hut
	Restrooms
	Restaurant/snacks
	Ski rentals ($9/day)
	Groomed trails
Admission:	$8
Dogs:	Pets NOT allowed
Hours:	9 AM to 5 PM
Contact:	Peek'n Peak
	1405 Olde Road, Box 360, Findley Lake, NY 14736
	www.pknpk.com
	(716) 355-4141

For Snow Conditions Call: (716) 355-4141

Peek'n Peak is a year-round resort, offering golf in the summer and downhill and cross-country skiing in the winter. Novice skiers will find over 4 miles of flat, easy, groomed trails on the valley floor across from the downhill ski area. Or head up to the more hilly terrain above the downhill area. Most of the trails are on the golf course, the exception being the Ravine Loop.

Cross-country ski passes can be purchased in the Annex Building. The ski touring office is in the back, facing the downhill ski slope.

	Trail Name	Distance	Level of Difficulty
A	Inner Loop	0.5 mile	Novice
B	Outer Loop	2.0 miles	Novice
C	Mid Golf Course	0.5 mile	Novice
D	Valley Trail	1.2 miles	Novice
1	South Hill Loop	1.4 miles	Intermediate
2	Upper Loop Trail	1.2 miles	Intermediate
3	Summit Trail	0.4 mile	Novice
4	Upper Ponds	0.7 mile	Novice
5	Ravine Loop	0.7 mile	Intermediate

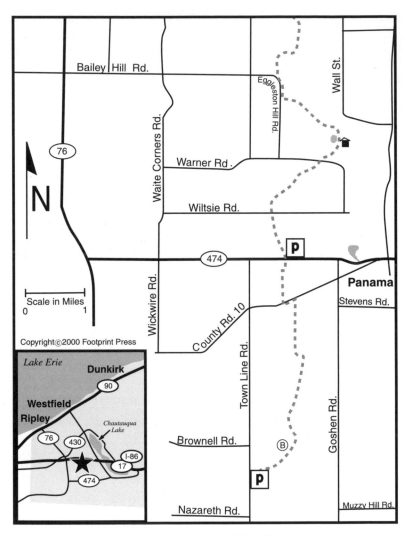

Westside Overland Trail (South Section)

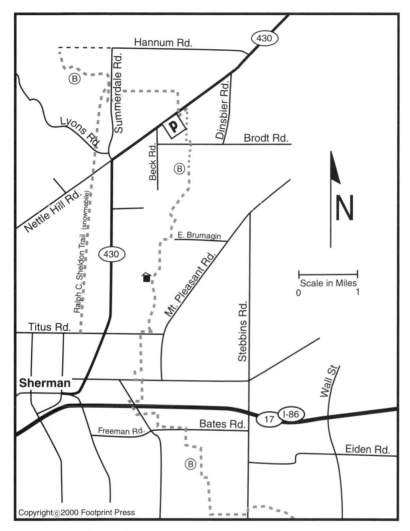

Westside Overland Trail (North Section)

2.

Westside Overland Trail

Location:	Sherman & Panama, Chautauqua County
Directions:	From Route 17 (I-86) take exit 6 at Sherman. For the southern parking area, head south on Route 76. Turn east onto Brownell Road, then south on Town Line Road. For the northern parking area, head north on Route 76 then take a right onto Route 430. Follow Route 430 to the parking area past Beck Road.
Length:	24 miles (one way)
Difficulty:	Intermediate
Terrain:	Mostly flat with some moderate hills
Trail Markings:	Blue blazes, wooden signs at road crossings and turns
Uses:	Skiing, Snowshoeing, Hiking
Amenities:	Shelters
	Groomed (1 mile section south of Route 430)
Admission:	Free
Dogs:	OK on leash
Hours:	Dawn to dusk
Contact:	Chautauqua County Parks
	2097 South Maple Street, Ashville, NY 14710
	(716) 763-8928

For Snow Conditions Call: No phone report

www.xcski.org, under daily snow report for New York

The Fred J. Cusimano Westside Overland Trail winds through State Forests, Chautauqua County land, and private property. Be sure to stay on the marked trail while on private property. It's mostly woodland with a few field areas. From the northern parking area on Route 430, the first mile heading south is groomed. The section south to Titus Road passes through NYS Reforestation Area land and is particularly nice in winter.

At the northern end you'll cross the Ralph C. Sheldon Trail. This is part of the Chautauqua Rails-to-Trails network but is a major thoroughfare for snowmobiles.

Trail Segment	Mileage
Southern parking area to Route 10	3.7 miles
Route 10 to Eggleston Hill Road	4.7 miles
Eggleston Hill Road to Bates Road	5.5 miles
Bates Road to Titus Road	2.4 miles
Titus Road to Brodt Road	3.8 miles
Brodt Road to Summerdale Road	2.3 miles
Summerdale Road to Hannum Road	1.5 miles

Friends on a Pack, Paddle, Ski snowshoe outing
enjoy a rest on an almost buried bench.

ALLEN S HILL

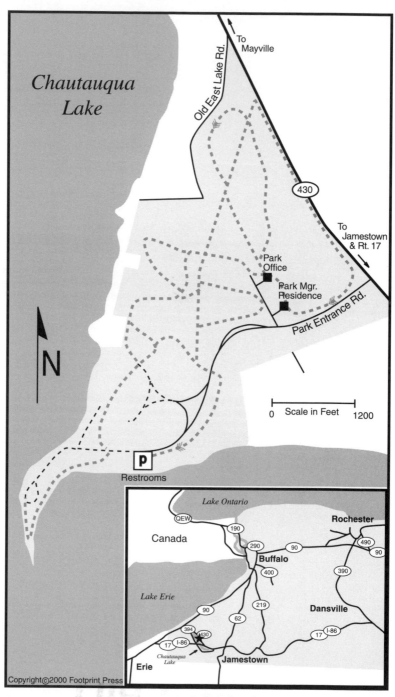

Chautauqua
Lake

To
Mayville

Old East Lake Rd.

430

To
Jamestown
& Rt. 17

Park
Office

Park Mgr.
Residence

Park Entrance Rd.

N

Scale in Feet
0   1200

P

Restrooms

Lake Ontario

QEW

190

Canada

290   90

Buffalo   490   90

400

390

Lake Erie

90   219

Dansville

62

394

17   I-86   430   17   I-86

Chautauqua
Lake

Erie   Jamestown

Rochester

Long Point State Park

3.
Long Point State Park

Location:	Lake Chautauqua, Chautauqua County
Directions:	From Route 17 (now I-86) take exit 10 and head north on Route 430. The entrance to the park will be on the left.
Length:	7 miles of trails
Difficulty:	Novice, Intermediate
Terrain:	Moderate hills
Trail Markings:	None
Uses:	Skiing, Snowshoeing, Snowmobiling, Hiking
Amenities:	Restrooms
Admission:	Free ($5-6/vehicle May through September)
Dogs:	OK on leash
Hours:	Dawn to dusk
Contact:	Long Point on Lake Chautauqua State Park 4459 Route 430, Bemus Point, NY 14712 (716) 386-2722

For Snow Conditions Call: (716) 386-2722

Lake Chautauqua sits at 1,308 feet above sea level, making it one of the highest navigable bodies of water in North America. Long Point, which juts peninsula-like into Lake Chautauqua, is one of the moraines left long ago by a retreating glacier.

The trails are ungroomed but get packed by snowmobiles. They wind through a heavy forest of beech, maple, spruce, poplar, and oak trees and jut to the very tip of Long Point.

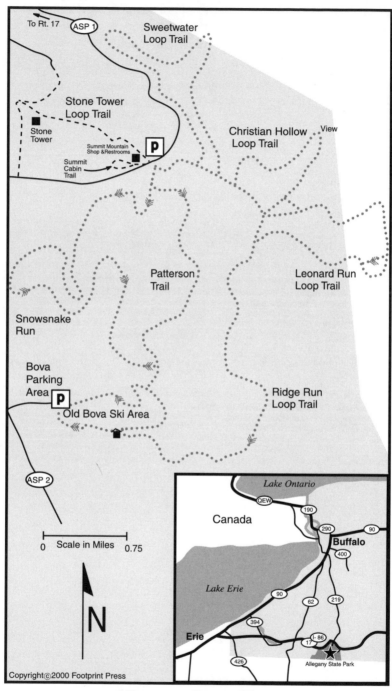

Allegany State Park

28 **Art Roscoe Cross-country Ski Area**

4.
Allegany State Park
Art Roscoe Cross-country Ski Area

Location: Salamanca, Cattaraugus County

Directions: From Route 17 (now I-86) take exit 21 at Salamanca and head south into Allegany State Park on ASP 1. Park at the Summit parking area.

Length: 24 miles of trails

Difficulty: Novice, Intermediate, Advanced

Terrain: Hilly

Trail Markings: Signs at the beginning of each trail. Degree of difficulty signs along trails.

Uses: Skiing, Snowshoeing

Amenities: Warming hut with snack bar (open weekends only)
Restrooms (in warming hut)
Groomed trails (double tracks)
Ski ($15/day) and snowshoe ($10/day) rentals provided by J-Con Concessions (716) 945 0523
Cabins for rent in winter, call 1-800-456-CAMP

Admission: Free during the week, $5/vehicle on weekends

Dogs: Pets NOT allowed

Hours: Dawn to dusk

Contact: Allegany State Park
2373 ASP Route 1, Suite 3, Salamanca, NY 14779
(716) 354-9101

For Snow Conditions Call: (716) 354-9163
www.xcski.org, under daily snow report for New York

At an elevation of 2,152 feet, this area enjoys an extended snow season, particularly on the high elevation trails of Sweetwater, Christian, and Leonard Run. These trails offer long climbs and descents on wide trails, and sweeping vistas. Ski-skating ("V" type skiing) is allowed only on Stone Tower Loop, Patterson, and Snowsnake Run Trails.

Trail	Distance	Level of Difficulty
Sweetwater Trail	2.7 mile loop	Novice
Christian Hollow Trail	1.6 mile loop	Intermediate
Crossover	0.2 miles	Intermediate
Leonard Run Trail	2.9 mile loop	Intermediate
Stone Tower Trail	2.3 mile loop	Intermediate
Snowsnake Run	4.9 miles	Advanced
Ridge Run Trail	3.3 mile loop	Intermediate
Patterson Trail	2.2 miles	Intermediate

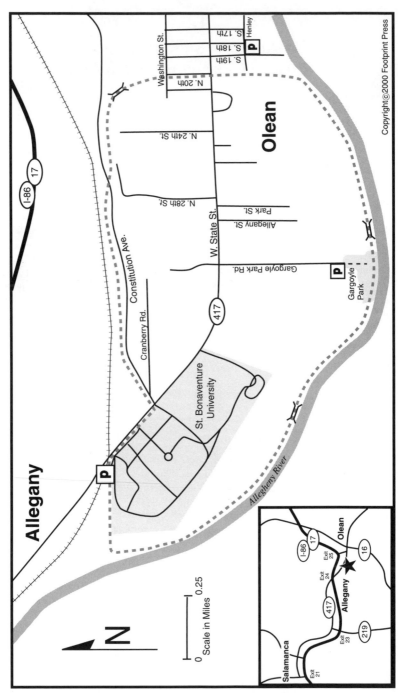

Allegheny River Valley Trail

5.

Allegheny River Valley Trail

Location: Allegany & Olean, Cattaraugus County

Directions: From Route 17 (now I-86) exit at Olean (exit 25). Follow Buffalo Street southeast toward Olean. Continue straight on N. 12th Street. Turn right (west) on State Street. Turn left (south) onto Gargoyle Park Road and follow it to the end.

Length: 5.6 mile loop

Difficulty: Novice

Terrain: Flat

Trail Markings: Large colorful "Allegheny River Valley Trail" signs

Uses: Skiing, Snowshoeing, Hiking

Amenities: None

(Restrooms are planned for Gargoyle Park in 2001.)

Admission: Free

Dogs: OK on leash

Hours: 24 hours

Contact: Greater Olean Area Chamber of Commerce
120 North Union Street, Olean, NY 14760
(716) 372-4433, email: tourism@oleanny.com
www.oleanny.com

For Snow Conditions Call: (716) 372-4433

This paved path winds through the diverse neighborhoods of Allegany, St. Bonaventure University, and Olean passing through residential, commercial, and college campus areas. It also follows the banks of the Allegheny River through woods. It's an easy, ungroomed trail, perfect for a crisp winter outing.

Distinctive signs
clearly mark the way
on the
Allegheny River Valley Trail.

Skip and Nicki Millor enjoy a winter day on the trails,
watching for skiers needing assistance
as part of the Nordic Ski Patrol.

Niagara
& Erie
Counties

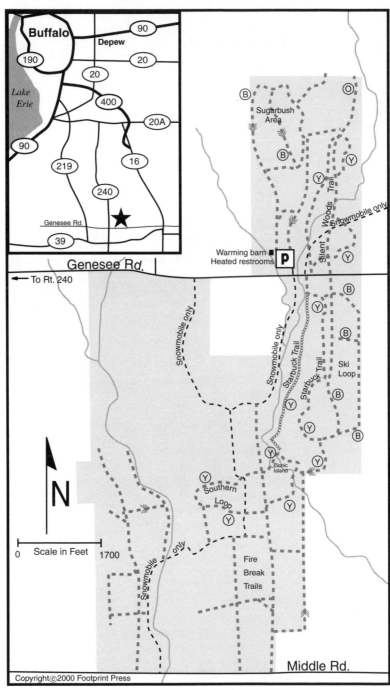

Erie County Forest

6.
Erie County Forest

Location:	Sardinia, Erie County
Directions:	Erie County Forest is in the southeast corner of Erie County, between Routes 240, 39, and 16. The parking area is on the north side of Genesee Road, midway between Routes 240 and 16.
Length:	15 miles of trails
Difficulty:	Novice, Intermediate, Advanced
Terrain:	Hilly
Trail Markings:	Yellow and blue blazes Conservation Trail - orange blazes
Uses:	Skiing, Snowshoeing, Hiking, Snowmobiling
Amenities:	Warming Hut Restrooms
Dogs:	OK on leash
Admission:	Free
Hours:	Dawn to dusk (closed during deer hunting season, late November to early December)
Contact:	County of Erie, Department of Parks, Recreation and Forestry 11929 Warner Gulf Road, East Concord, NY 14055 (716) 496-7410

For Snow Conditions Call: (716) 496-7410 or (716) 858-8351

Erie County Forest sits at high elevation where snow comes early and is plentiful. There's a broad network of trails including dirt roads, fire break trails, and woodland trails. In summer bicycles enjoy most of the trails except the yellow-blazed hiking trails:

Silent Woods Trail - 1.75 mile loop north of Genesee Road (Advanced)
Scarbuck Trail - 1.75 mile loop south of Genesee Road (Intermediate)
Southern Loop - 1.25 mile loop south of Scarbuck Trail (Intermediate)

You'll also find orange blazes as the Conservation Trail (part of the Finger Lakes Trail System) snakes through Erie County Forest.

In winter, the dirt roads become a snowmobile trail. Skiers and snowshoers should avoid this trail. Snowshoeing is allowed on any other trail. Skiing is allowed on all but the western most leg of the Scarbuck Trail. Washouts have left some steep sections, hard to traverse on skis.

There are two blue-blazed novice ski trail areas. On the north side of Genesee Road is the Sugarbush Area. The trails take you quickly uphill to a windswept plateau. The 2-mile ski loop on the south side of Genesee Road offers a wide trail through a pine forest. Head deeper into the south side and you'll find lots of variety, with some steep hills and narrow bridges.

A sugar shanty and sawmill are located near the parking area. Tours are offered through the working sugar shanty (producing maple syrup) and sawmill during March and April from 9 AM until 3 PM.

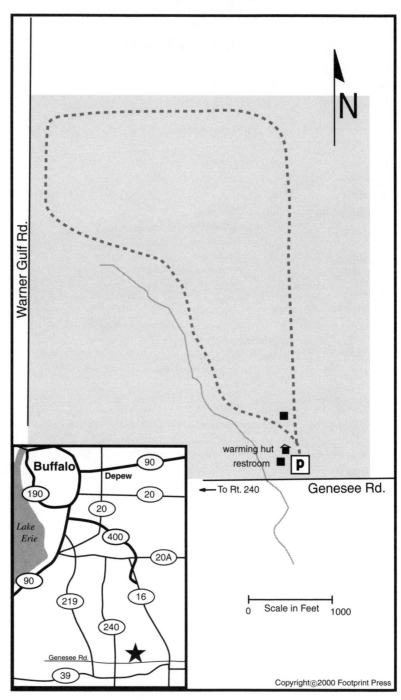

Erie County Forest - Lot 3

7.

Erie County Forest - Lot 3

Location:	Sardinia, Erie County
Directions:	Erie County Forest is in the southeast corner of Erie County, between Routes 240, 39, and 16. The parking area is on the north side of Genesee Road, east of Warner Gulf Road.
Length:	3 mile loop
Difficulty:	Intermediate
Terrain:	Hilly
Trail Markings:	Large sign, skier on brown background
Uses:	Skiing, Snowshoeing
Amenities:	Warming Hut
	Outhouse
Dogs:	OK on leash
Admission:	Free
Hours:	Dawn to dusk (closed during deer hunting season, late November to early December)
Contact:	County of Erie, Department of Parks, Recreation and Forestry 11929 Warner Gulf Road, East Concord, NY 14055 (716) 496-7410

For Snow Conditions Call: (716) 496-7410 or (716) 858-8351

This area is only open during winter. In fact, the gate to the parking area is kept locked until there's enough snow to ski. In summer it's a wet area. This makes it a pristine forest for winter enjoyment.

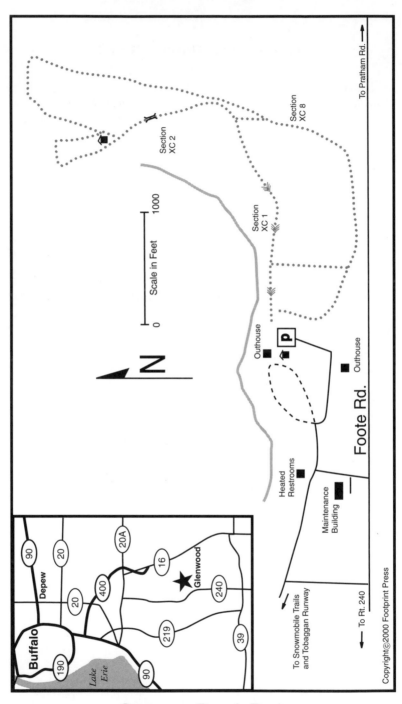

Sprague Brook Park

8.

Sprague Brook Park

Location:	Glenwood, Erie County
Directions:	From Buffalo, follow Route 240 south. Past Glenwood, turn east on Foote Road and use the second entrance to Sprague Brook Park.
Length:	3 mile loop
Difficulty:	Novice, Intermediate
Terrain:	Mild hills
Trail Markings:	Red & yellow metal ski signs
	Red & white arrow signs in woods
Uses:	Skiing, Snowshoeing
Amenities:	Warming Hut
	Outhouse
	Groomed
Dogs:	OK on leash
Admission:	Free
Hours:	Dawn to dusk
Contact:	County of Erie, Department of Parks, Recreation and Forestry
	Sprague Brook Park
	Foote Road, Glenwood, NY 14069
	(716) 592-2804

For Snow Conditions Call: (716) 858-8513

Sprague Brook Park offers a groomed ski trail, perfect for the skater or novice skier. It's a 3-mile loop that's well marked and easy to follow on gentle grades through a beautiful forest. The trails in the western end of the park are designated for snowmobiles—far from the ski trail. The park also offers year-round camping facilities.

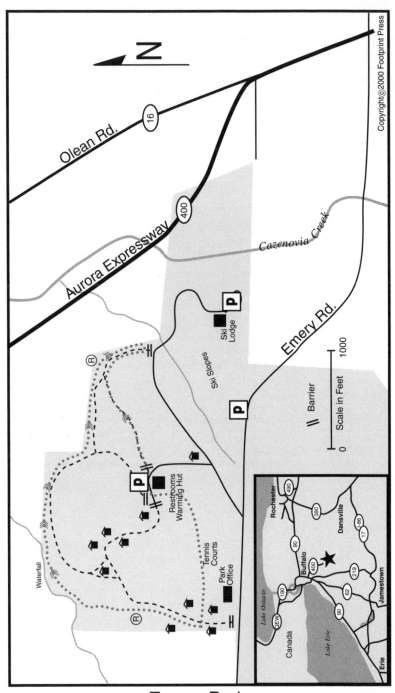

Emery Park

9.

Emery Park

Location:	South Wales, Erie County
Directions:	From Buffalo, head east on Route 400 until it turns into Route 16. Turn west onto Emery Road and drive one mile to the park entrance on the right.
Length:	1.6 mile loop trail
	Additional unplowed roads
Difficulty:	Intermediate
Terrain:	Hilly
Trail Markings:	Red blazes, red wooden arrows, large skier sign
Uses:	Skiing, Snowshoeing, Hiking
	Snowmobiling (south of Emery Road)
Amenities:	Warming hut (Field House)
	Restrooms
	Groomed
Dogs:	OK on leash
Admission:	Free
Hours:	Dawn to dusk
Contact:	County of Erie, Department of Parks, Recreation and Forestry
	Emery Park
	2084 Emery Road, South Wales, NY 14139
	(716) 652-1380

For Snow Conditions Call: (716) 652-1380

There are two sections to this park, bisected by Emery Road. The southern portion has the snowmobile trail. The northern section (shown on the map) is for skiers and snowshoers. Several roads are blocked and unplowed in winter making them part of the groomed network of trails. The main trail leaves from the Field House (warming hut with rest rooms), crosses a flat play field then winds through the woods passing a deep gorge and spectacular waterfall. The path is wide but it's a long downhill heading out and a long uphill on the return portion of the loop. Follow the unplowed roads for a less strenuous return.

Novices can ski here. Just stay on the more level terrain near the Field House and the unplowed roads. Or, head to the south side of the park. Just beware of snowmobiles. The park also has a T-bar serving a small downhill ski slope.

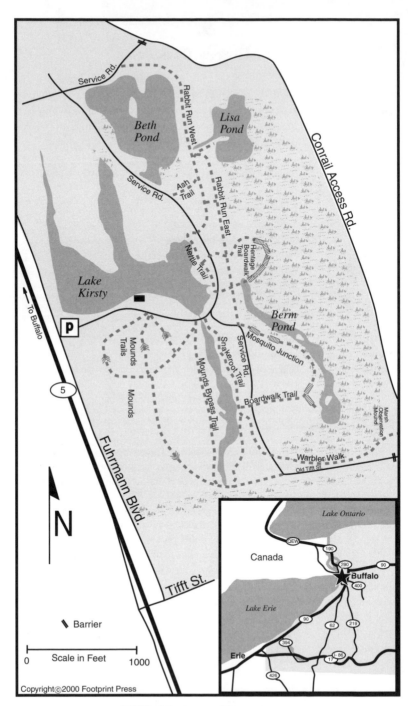

Tifft Nature Preserve

10.

Tifft Nature Preserve

Location:	Buffalo, Erie County
Directions:	From downtown Buffalo, head south on the skyway (Route 5). Take the Tifft Street exit. Turn left onto Tifft Street, then left again onto Fuhrmann Blvd. Tifft Nature Preserve will be on the right.
Length:	5 miles of trails
Difficulty:	Novice
Terrain:	Mostly flat, mild hills in mounds area
Trail Markings:	None
Uses:	Skiing, Snowshoeing, Hiking
Amenities:	Warming Hut (nature center)
	Hot & cold drinks available
	Gift shop
	Restrooms
	Snowshoe rentals ($3/hour)
Dogs:	Pets NOT allowed
Admission:	Free (donations suggested)
Hours:	Dawn to dusk
Contact:	Tifft Nature Preserve
	1200 Fuhrmann Boulevard, Buffalo, NY 14203
	(716) 825-6397

For Snow Conditions Call: (716) 825-6397

The lands of Tifft Nature Preserve have a long history. Originally a food gathering place for local Indians, the land was purchased by George Washington Tifft in the 1880s. He used the area for dairy farming and stockyards. In the late 1900s the Lehigh Valley Railroad built a rail/canal complex. In 1972 the city of Buffalo purchased the land for a secondary sewage treatment plant on Squaw Island. The solid waste produced made the 4 mounds that were covered with soil and are skiable today.

The land is now operated by the Buffalo Museum of Science. They operate the Makowski Visitor Center with exhibits, tables, and restrooms. The center is open daily from 9 AM until 5 PM except on Mondays. The trails are open every day from dawn to dusk. Snowshoes can be rented in the visitor center.

Skiing the open mounds affords a view of Lake Erie and downtown Buffalo. Or, choose the flat woods trails to the frozen ponds and marshlands. The day we explored the trails Canada geese wandered the trails, oblivious to our presence.

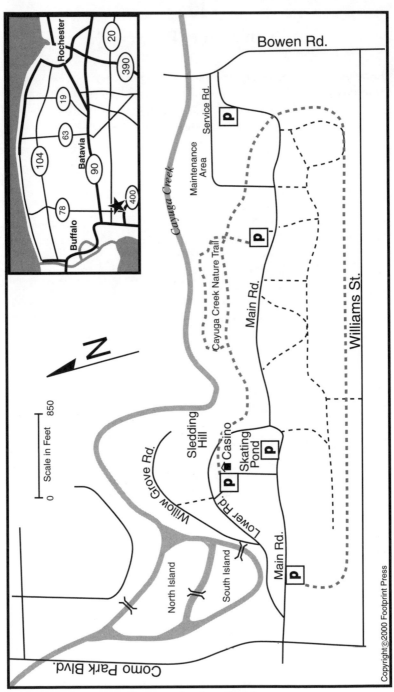

Como Lake Park

11.

Como Lake Park

Location:	Lancaster, Erie County
Directions:	From Route 20 (Broadway), east of Lancaster, head south on Bowen Road. Turn west into Como Lake Park. Park at any of the four designated winter parking areas (see map).
Length:	0.75 mile Nature Trail
	4 miles of trails and unplowed roads
Difficulty:	Novice
Terrain:	Mostly flat. Nature Trail loops off the upland section to the lower floodplain of Cayuga Creek.
Trail Markings:	None
Uses:	Skiing, Hiking
Amenities:	Warming hut (Casino shelter)
	Restrooms (Casino shelter)
Dogs:	OK on leash
Admission:	Free
Hours:	Dawn to dusk
Contact:	County of Erie Department of Parks, Recreation & Forestry
	Como Lake Park
	Como Park Blvd., Lancaster, NY 14086
	(716) 683-5430

For Snow Conditions Call: (716) 683-5430

All the skiing here is easy but scenic. You can select a route for length and view. The Nature Trail runs from the Boy Scout Shelter, downhill to the floodplain of Cayuga Creek then climbs back to the upland plain where most of Como Lake Park is situated.

You can circumnavigate the park on the designated ski route or wander freely on the unplowed roads or even cross the bridges onto South and North Islands, nestled in Cayuga Creek.

To warm up or visit a restroom, stop at the Casino. You won't find slot machines. The Casino is a warming hut with a big fireplace, situated between a skating rink and sledding hill. It can be a hive of activity of on a beautiful winter day.

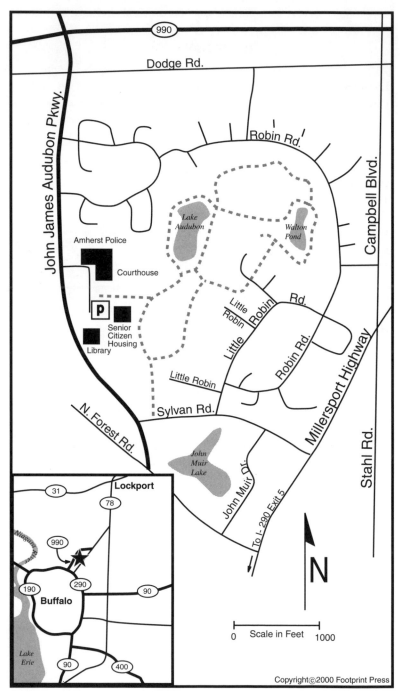

Walton Woods

12.

Walton Woods

Location:	Amherst, Erie County
Directions:	From Interstate 290, take exit 5 to head north on Millersport Highway. Turn left (west) on North Forest Road, then right (north) on John James Audubon Parkway. Park in the public lot for the Town of Amherst (courthouse, police, library).
Length:	2.3 miles of trail
Difficulty:	Novice
Terrain:	Flat
Trail Markings:	None
Uses:	Skiing, Snowshoeing, Hiking
Amenities:	None
Dogs:	OK
Admission:	Free
Hours:	Dawn to dusk
Contact:	Town of Amherst Recreation Department 1615 Amherst Manor Drive, Amherst, NY 14221 (716) 631-7132

For Snow Conditions Call: (716) 631-7132

The easy trails are adjacent to the Audubon housing development. They wind through woods and around Audubon Lake and Walton Pond. From the Town of Amherst parking area, find the trailhead south of the courthouse/police station building.

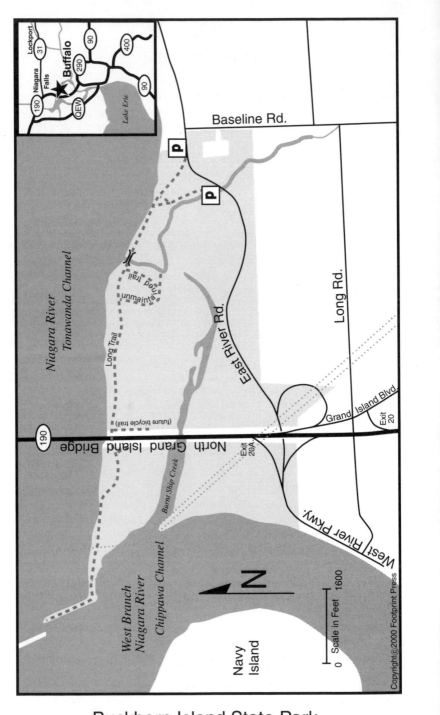

Buckhorn Island State Park

13.

Buckhorn Island State Park

Location:	Grand Island, Erie County
Directions:	If heading south on I-190, take exit 20A. Turn left and follow East River Road to the parking areas. If traveling north on I-190, take exit 20. Turn west on Long Road, then right (N) on West River Parkway. This will turn into East River Road and lead to the parking areas.
Length:	Long Trail - 5.1 miles round trip
	Unmaintained side loop - 0.5 mile
Difficulty:	Novice
Terrain:	Flat
Trail Markings:	None (a portion of the trail is orange blazed as part of the FLT Conservation Trail)
Uses:	Skiing, Snowshoeing, Hiking
Amenities:	None
Dogs:	OK on leash (must clean up after pet)
Admission:	Free
Hours:	Dawn to dusk
Contact:	Buckhorn Island State Park
	c/o Beaver Island State Park
	2136 West Oakfield Road, Grand Island, NY 14072
	(716) 773-3271

For Snow Conditions Call: (716) 773-3271

Buckhorn Island State Park sits at the northwest point of Grand Island. It's an island by virtue of Burnt Ship Creek which bisects this 895 acres of marsh, meadows, and woods. The Long Trail leads along the shoreline of the Niagara River, under the North Grand Island Bridge, to the tip of a jetty. It affords great views of the river, other shorelines, marshes, many flocks of resident geese, ducks, and gulls.

The Niagara River corridor was officially designated an "Important Bird Area" in December, 1996. Nineteen species of gulls have been found here, representing almost half of the world's 45 species. The area is also on the migration route for 25 species of waterfowl. Many even overwinter along the river. That makes a winter trip to Buckhorn Island State Park a special treat. The most numerous gulls found here are Bonaparte's gull, ring-billed gull, and herring gull. The most common waterfowl to be found are greater scaup, common mergansers, and canvasbacks. Be sure to take your binoculars.

Buckhorn Island State Park is slated for major improvements beginning in 2001, designed to make the park more accessible and to improve wildlife viewing. The improvements include additional observation areas, parking areas, and trails. A trail specifically designed for bicycles will be built, with access from North Grand Island Bridge.

The trail at Buckhorn Island State Park
parallels the Niagara River.

**Dirty snow
melts faster
than clean snow.**

Orleans, Genesee & Wyoming Counties

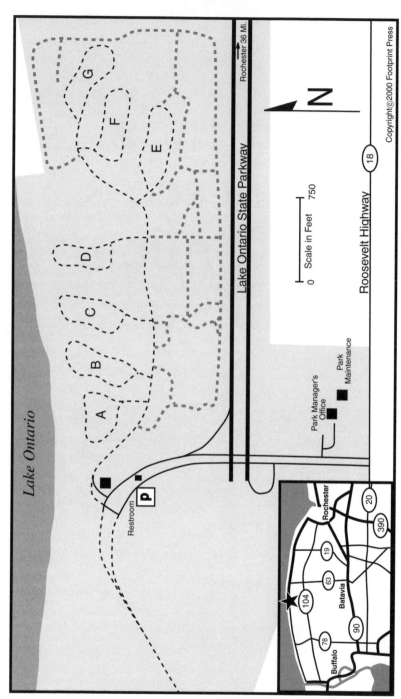

Lakeside Beach State Park

14.

Lakeside Beach State Park

Location:	Waterport, Orleans County
Directions:	Take the Lake Ontario State Parkway to it's western end and head north to the parking area.
Length:	3 miles of trails
	3 miles of unplowed roads
Difficulty:	Novice
Terrain:	Gentle hills
Trail Markings:	None
Uses:	Skiing, Snowshoeing, Hiking
Amenities:	Restroom
Admission:	Free October to May ($5/vehicle rest of year)
Dogs:	OK on leash
Hours:	Dawn to dusk
Contact:	Lakeside Beach State Park
	Waterport, NY 14571
	(716) 682-4888

For Snow Conditions Call: (716) 682-4888

From the parking area, head east past the park manager's house. The dogs bark but they're friendly. Bear right to find the trailhead. The trails are four-feet wide mowed swaths through a mixture of tall grasses, shrubs, and trees. Because the forest isn't dense, we found ourselves enjoying the graceful and varied shapes of the large trees silhouetted against the sky as we skied. The other option in this park is to follow the unplowed roads through the summer camping areas which are labeled A, B, C, etc.

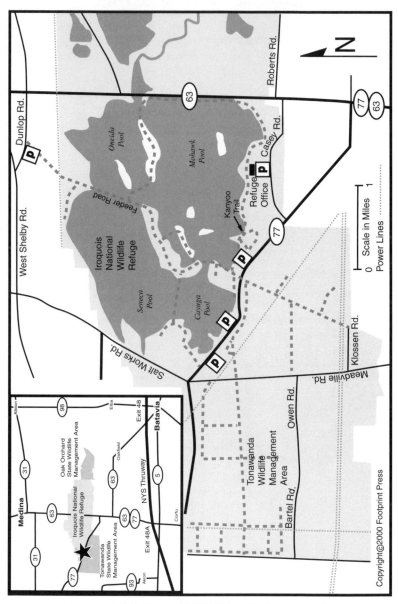

Iroquois National Wildlife Refuge and
Tonawanda Wildlife Management Area

15.

Iroquois National Wildlife Refuge and Tonawanda Wildlife Management Area

Location:	Alabama, Genesee & Orleans Counties
Directions:	Park at the Iroquois National Wildlife Refuge office at 1101 Casey Road which runs between Routes 77 and 63. None of the parking areas shown on the map are plowed on weekends.
Length:	30 miles of trails
Difficulty:	Novice, Intermediate
Terrain:	Flat
Trail Markings:	Ski trail has markers, none on dikes & service roads
Uses:	Skiing, Snowshoeing, Hiking
Amenities:	Porta-potty at Kanyoo Trail parking area
Admission:	Free
Dogs:	OK on leash
Hours:	Dawn to dusk
Contacts:	Iroquois National Wildlife Refuge 1101 Casey Road, Basom, NY 14013 (716) 948-5445
	NYS Department of Environmental Conservation 6274 E. Avon-Lima Road, Avon, NY 14414 (716) 226-2466 http://www.dec.state.ny.us

For Snow Conditions Call: None

Iroquois National Wildlife Refuge and Tonawanda Wildlife Management Area join together with Oak Orchard Wildlife Management Area to form a total of 19,000 acres of impounded marshlands for the nurturing of wildlife.

The official ski trail is a 7.5-mile loop around Mohawk Pool. It begins behind the refuge office at 1101 Casey Road. The ski trail is managed for wildlife nesting during summer months and is closed after March 1st. The Kanyoo Trail is a narrow 1-mile loop trail that is open year round. Feeder Road is a 3.5-mile gravel path which once was the main road between Medina and Akron but is now closed to motorized traffic. Finally, there is a network of raised dikes, and service roads south of Route 77 which are available for winter activities on skis or snowshoes.

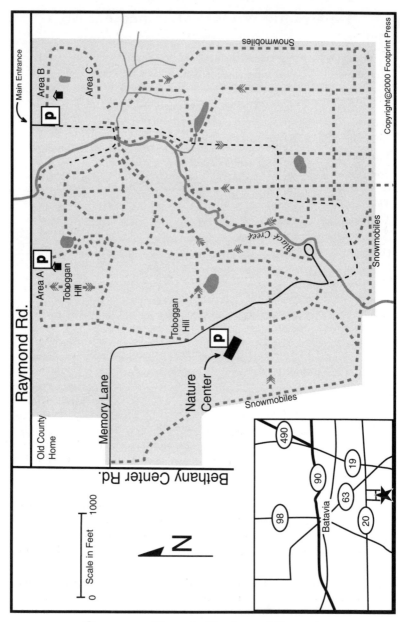

Genesee County Park and Forest

16.

Genesee County Park and Forest

Location:	Bethany (south of Batavia), Genesee County
Directions:	From Route 20, turn south on Bethany Center Road. Turn east on Raymond Road. Park on the right in Areas A or B.
Length:	6 miles of trails
Difficulty:	Novice, Intermediate
Terrain:	Hilly
Trail Markings:	Some junction number signs and some trail name signs
Uses:	Skiing, Snowshoeing, Hiking, Snowmobiling
Amenities:	Warming hut (nature center)
	Restrooms (nature center)
	Groomed trails
Admission:	Free
Dogs:	OK on leash
Hours:	May 1-Sept. 30: 9 AM-9 PM
	Oct.1-April 30: 9 AM-5 PM
Contact:	Genesee County Park and Forest
	11095 Bethany Center Road, East Bethany, NY 14054
	(716) 344-1122

For Snow Conditions Call: (716) 344-1122

Genesee County Park and Forest is the first and oldest county forest in New York State and owes its existence to a home for the poor. Some of the old buildings can still be seen on the corner of Bethany Center Road and Raymond Road.

In 1882, the county purchased a wood lot to supply the cooking and heating needs of the "Poor House Farm" and sold wood for $0.75 a cord to cover expenses. In 1915, about 31,000 trees were planted at a cost of $225. These trees were the beginning of the establishment of the forest. More evergreens were planted in the 1920s, and 169,000 trees had been planted by 1935. The land was designated the first county forest in New York State. The Genesee County Park and Forest became a reality in 1971.

This park covers 44 acres of rolling hills that are criss-crossed with trails. More importantly, it lies at the easternmost end of the lake-effect snow plume that blows off Lake Erie. Genesee County Park will have snow when areas just east of it are snowless. Park personnel pack the trails with a snowmobile to provide easy skiing. It is recommended that skiers stay off the perimeter trail which is used by snowmobilers.

In 1998, a group from Job Corps joined local volunteers to build a stunning nature center complete with stuffed animals and natural exhibits. They now offer a variety of nature programs. Stop in to pick up a schedule. The nature center is open:

May 1-Sept. 30:	3 PM-6 PM weekdays, Noon-6 PM weekends
Nov.-April 30:	3 PM-5 PM weekdays, Noon-5 PM weekends

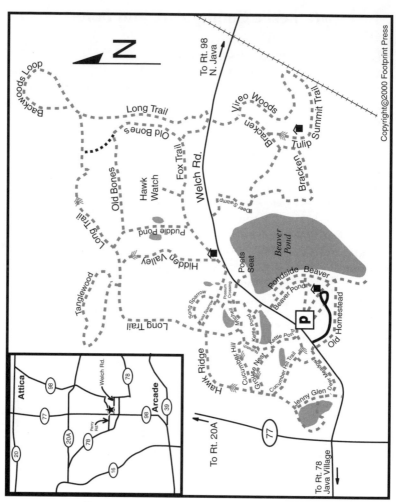

Beaver Meadow Audubon Center

17.

Beaver Meadow Audubon Center

Location:	North Java, Wyoming County
Directions:	From the New York State Thruway, follow Route 98 south. Turn right (W) on Perry Road, then left on Welch Road. Follow the signs to the Nature Center parking area. Or, from Route 17, turn east on Welsh Road and follow the signs to the Nature Center parking area.
Length:	8 miles of loop trails
Difficulty:	Novice, Intermediate
Terrain:	Gentle hills
Trail Markings:	Well-labeled by brown wooden signs with yellow lettering
Uses:	Skiing, Snowshoeing, Hiking
Amenities:	Warming hut (nature center)
	Gift shop
	Restrooms (in nature center) & outhouses
	Snowshoe rentals
Admission:	A donation is requested ($2 per person or $5 per family)
Dogs:	Pets NOT allowed
Hours:	Trails are open 24 hours/day
Contact:	Beaver Meadow Audubon Center
	Buffalo Audubon Society, Inc.
	1610 Welch Road, North Java, NY 14113-9713
	(716) 457-3228

For Snow Conditions Call: (716) 457-3228

Beaver Meadow Audubon Center is a 324-acre wildlife preserve which has been developed by the Buffalo Audubon Society. The visitor center has seasonal exhibits, live animals, a discovery room, and a library. It is open year round, Tuesday through Saturday from 10 AM-5 PM, and Sundays 1 PM-5 PM. It is closed Mondays and major holidays.

This area is busy year-round. In the winter, lake-effect snow dumps off Lake Erie making it a winter playground. Snowshoes can be rented for a challenging romp along the trails. Maple sugar is made in the sugarhouse in early spring.

Many loops are available within the network of trails. Intersections are well labeled so you can create your own adventure by following the map. To find less heavily traveled areas, head back to the Long Trail, Tanglewood Trail, and Backwoods Loop Trail. Or wander south of Welch Road on Deer Swamp Trail, Bracken Trail, Tulip Summit Trail, and Vireo Woods Trail.

Backwoods Loop Trail – Follow the orange bands on the trees to stay on this less frequently traveled loop through the woods.

Beaver Meadow Audubon Center continued:

Beaver Pond Trail – Glide through the woods along the beaver pond. The trail leads to a dead-end at the beaver dam and beaver house so you can actually reach out and touch them. There are interpretive signs about beavers, chipmunks, and woodchucks along the way, and an observation platform overlooking the pond.

Chipmunk Run – A short connector trail that winds through the woods.

Cucumber Hill Trail – This trail passes a cross section of a 350-year old eastern hemlock tree and a set of outhouses.

Deer Meadow Trail – Follow this trail through the woods to circle a meadow, then return to woods. An interpretive sign assists with bird identification along the way.

Deer Swamp Trail – A woods trail with switchbacks to a boardwalk through a swamp. The trail continues through the woods and along a pond.

Field Sparrow Trail – As the name implies, this is a trail through a field.

Fox Trail – Follow this path through a scrub field to the young arboretum. There is a spur trail to the hawk watch area.

Grouse Nest Trail – This trail is harder to follow than most as it winds through the woods. The adventurous are rewarded with an overlook to the kettle pond.

Hawk Ridge Trail – A woods wander.

Hidden Valley Trail – The southern end starts in a young arboretum then ventures through a small woods to a valley between small hills.

Jenny Glen Boardwalk – A quarter mile boardwalk with railings over wetland and woods.

Kettle Pond Trail – Follow this path over two small wooden bridges and around a kettle pond which will be hidden under white in winter. Kettle ponds such as this one were created when a large block of ice separated from the glacier. Water running off the glacier deposited gravel and debris all around the ice block. The block eventually melted, leaving behind a rough circular depression filled with water. An interpretive sign on this trail will help identify small aquatic animals.

Long Trail – This is a hilly trail on a ridge through the woods and scrub apple trees. Along the way you'll cross some wooden bridges and boardwalks.

Mitchell Trail – A trail through pines and mixed wood forest. Cross a wooden bridge along the way.

Nuthatch Trail – This is a connector trail through a pine forest. It has a bird observation area.

Old Bones Trail – A woods trail.

Old Woods Bracken Trail – Glide through an old woods forest with a high canopy.

Poet's Seat – A short trail down to a bench and pond view. Sit and reflect awhile.

Pondside Trail – This path parallels the pond and goes to a lookout at a covered observation shelter. There are some steps (steep sections) along this hilly path.

Possum Crossing Trail – Ski through the woods to a bench with a pond overlook. You'll end at a young arboretum.

Puddle Pond Trail – For a short distance, follow the path through scrub apple trees. The area will open into field then passes through the young arboretum.

Shadow Hill Trail – Wander through the woods with pine trees on one side of the trail and deciduous trees on the other. There are some steps (steep sections) along the way.

Tanglewood Trail – A less frequently traveled loop through the woods.

Tulip Summit Trail – Climb to a covered pavilion with benches; a mighty elevation of 150 feet. Nearby is a large tulip tree.

Vireo Woods Trail – Imagine the summer sound of vireos as you wander these woods. You'll cross a wooden bridge over Grouse Brook and pass a cabin on your way to Welsh Road.

Allan Muskopf's shadow follows him on a sunny day of skiing.

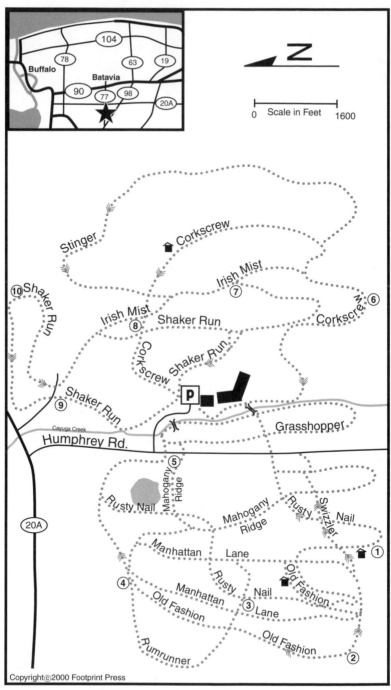

Byrncliff Resort & Conference Center

18.
Bryncliff Resort & Conference Center

Location:	Varysburg, Wyoming County
Directions:	From Route 20A between Routes 77 and 98, turn south on Humphrey Road.
Length:	12 miles of trails
	4 miles of lighted trail for night skiing
Difficulty:	Novice, Intermediate, Advanced
Terrain:	Hilly
Trail Markings:	Trail name signs and difficulty markers
	Numbered signs along trails help skiers establish where they are on the map
Uses:	Skiing, Snowshoeing
Amenities:	Warming hut (ski lodge) and shelters on trails
	Restrooms (in lodge)
	Restaurant, snacks
	Ski & snowshoe rentals ($8-9/day)
	Groomed trails
Admission:	$5 Tuesday - Friday
	$8 Friday - Sunday & Holidays
	Children under 10, free
Dogs:	Pets NOT allowed
Hours:	Monday 9 AM - 4 PM, Tuesday - Saturday 9 AM - 11 PM, Sunday 9 AM - 8 PM
Contact:	Bryncliff Resort & Conference Center Route 20A, Varysburg, NY 14167 www.bryncliff.com/cross.htm (716) 535-7300

For Snow Conditions Call: (716) 535-7300

Yes, Bryncliff is a golf resort during the summer but don't be turned off by the "skiing on a golf course" stigma. The ski trails of Bryncliff cross the golf course but they head up the hillsides into deep woods for the majority of their mileage.

We reached Bryncliff in late afternoon and headed out in daylight but spent most of our time skiing the trails in darkness. It was a fun and even romantic experience. Most of the trails on the west side of Humphrey Road are lighted for night skiing. We found the unlighted trails to be fun at night, too. The moon wasn't showing through heavy cloud cover but the glow off the blanket of white snow was enough to light our way. We weaved up and down through the woodland trails with ease.

The Bryncliff lodge is nestled in the valley between two hillsides. From the lodge the trails head generally uphill in each direction. This means you don't have to be a slave to a map to have a sense of where you are. Skiing can be carefree.

Bryncliff Resort continued:

The trails are groomed and many are track-set along the edge so you can choose between skiing a track or skating. Two new shelters were added in 2000. Each has an outdoor grille for picnics and a pit for bonfires. Bryncliff has lodging and a restaurant. They offer special overnight and dinner packages and events.

Trail	Distance	Level of Difficulty
West side:		
Rusty Nail	2.4 miles	Novice
Manhattan Lane	1.9 miles	Novice
Mahogany Ridge	1.5 miles	Novice
Rum Runner	1.7 miles	Intermediate
Old Fashion	1.4 miles	Intermediate
Swizzler	0.4 mile	Advanced
East side:		
Irish Mist	0.8 mile	Novice
Shaker Run	2.4 miles	Novice
Stinger	2.1 miles	Intermediate
Corkscrew	2.8 miles	Advanced

Monroe
County

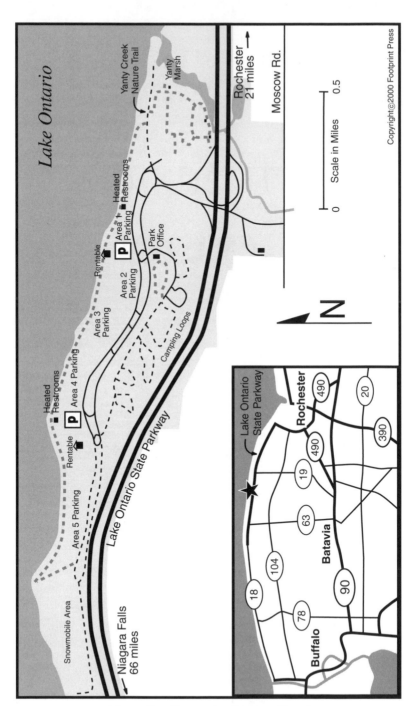

Copyright©2000 Footprint Press

Hamlin Beach State Park

19.

Hamlin Beach State Park

Location:	Hamlin, Monroe County
Directions:	From Rochester take Lake Ontario State Parkway west to the Hamlin Beach State Park exit.
Length:	5 miles of trails
	5 miles of unplowed roads
Difficulty:	Novice
Terrain:	Flat
Trail Markings:	Large brown and yellow signs mark the parking and camping areas
	None on trails
Uses:	Skiing, Snowshoeing, Hiking, Snowmobiling
Amenities:	Restrooms
Admission:	Free ($5-6/vehicle May through September)
Dogs:	OK on leash
Hours:	Dawn to dusk
Contact:	Hamlin Beach State Park
	Hamlin, NY 14464
	(716) 964-2462

For Snow Conditions Call: (716) 964-2462

In winter, Lake Ontario metamorphoses from moving water to an erie stillness of ice heaves and blow holes. Hamlin Beach State Park provides a front row seat to this icy winter spectacle. You can ski a trail along the shore or duck back into woods to follow a nature trail or the unplowed roads through the camping areas.

Winter camping is available in one area for the more hardy souls. The other areas are left unplowed and offer 2 miles of loops through a pine forest. Snowmobiles play west of Area 5 Parking, but the rest of the park is playground for us slower moving folk. At the far eastern end is the Yanty Creek Nature Trail. This is a 1.2 mile loop through high scrub and young forest. Observation platforms along the way offer views of the frozen creek and swamp areas.

Trail	Distance
Camping Loops	3 miles
Shoreline Trail	3.5 miles
Yanty Creek Trail	1.2 mile loop

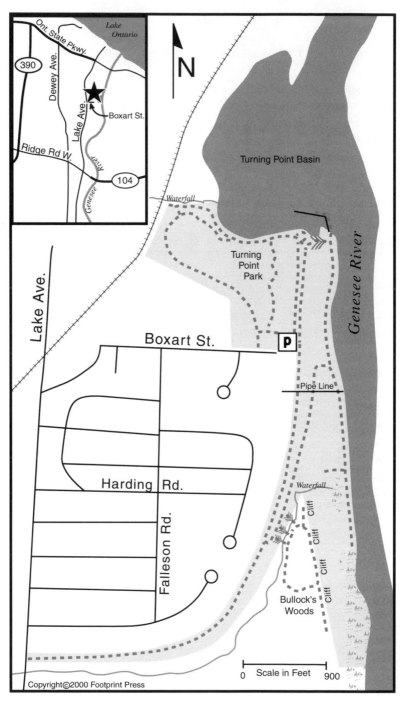

Turning Point Park &
Bullock's Woods Preserve

20.
Turning Point Park & Bullock's Woods Preserve

Location:	Charlotte, Monroe County
Directions:	From Lake Avenue (south of Stonewood Road), turn east on Boxart Street. Park at the end of Boxart Street.
Length:	4 miles of trails
Difficulty:	Intermediate
Terrain:	Some steep hills that can be avoided
Trail Markings:	None
Uses:	Skiing, Snowshoeing, Hiking
Amenities:	None
Admission:	Free
Dogs:	OK on leash
Hours:	Dawn to dusk
Contact:	Department of Parks, Recreation & Human Services City of Rochester 400 Dewey Avenue, Rochester, NY 14613 (716) 428-6770

For Snow Conditions Call: None

Turning Point Park is a 112-acre wilderness setting in an urban environment. The term "Turning Point" has double meaning to the Charlotte residents nearby. Historically, the wide basin in the nearby Genesee River was a physical place where ships could turn around before encountering the Lower Falls. This was once a heavily used industrial area with ships visiting docks to load and unload coal, wheat, feldspar, paper boxes, and tourists. An active cement plant still operates on this site.

In 1972 the Rochester-Monroe County Port Authority announced plans to build an oil storage tank farm on the site. Area residents, led by Bill Davis fought the plan which would have bulldozed a stand of 200-year-old oak trees and cut off community access to the river. They achieved a "Turning Point" in getting the city to turn away from commercial development of the river waterfront and toward its recreational use. The city bought the land in 1976 and opened Turning Point Park in 1977.

From the parking area, your journey will start high on a cliff with panoramic views of the river valley below. The long trails heading north/south are old railroad beds with gradual grades. Along the river you'll pass a series of docks, both active and abandoned.

Entering the Bullock's Woods Trail loop requires a short, steep downhill to cross the creek. The area to the northwest of the parking area has wide, easy trails through a forest with 200-year-old oak trees. Thanks Bill Davis, for having the foresight to fight for this urban treasure.

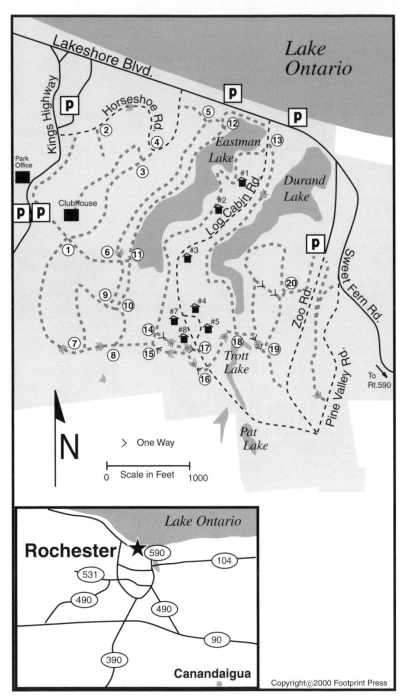

Durand Eastman Park

21.
Durand Eastman Park

Location:	Irondequoit, Monroe County
Directions:	Lakeshore Boulevard parallels the Lake Ontario shore in Irondequoit, north of Rochester. From Lakeshore Blvd., turn south on King's Highway and park at the clubhouse parking area.
Length:	5.5 miles of trails & unplowed roads
Difficulty:	Novice, Intermediate
Terrain:	Moderate hills
Trail Markings:	Some blue-and-white numbered signs on posts at trail junctions, some ski markers
Uses:	Skiing, Snowshoeing
Amenities:	Shelters
Admission:	Free
Dogs:	Pets NOT allowed
Hours:	Dawn to dusk
Contact:	Monroe County Parks Department 171 Reservoir Avenue, Rochester, NY 14620 (716) 256-4950

For Snow Conditions Call: None

The ski routes in this park traverse a combination of summertime golf course and woodland hiking trails. They offer long, steep curving downhill runs and open meadow skiing. The trails even parallel four small lakes.

The majority of trails are novice trails. The only advanced section is the east side of Durand Lake between markers 18 and 20.

Durand Eastman Park is known for its deer population. Many debates and attempts to cull the herd have occurred over the years. It's quite common to see deer year-round.

In 1907 George Eastman and Dr. Henry Durand gifted Durand's 484-acre estate to be used as a park. It included 4,000 feet of beachfront property. Over the years a large bath house was built and train tracks were laid to bring throngs of people from Rochester to enjoy a day at the beach. Today the bath house and train tracks are gone but many Rochesterians still enjoy the white sand beach in summer.

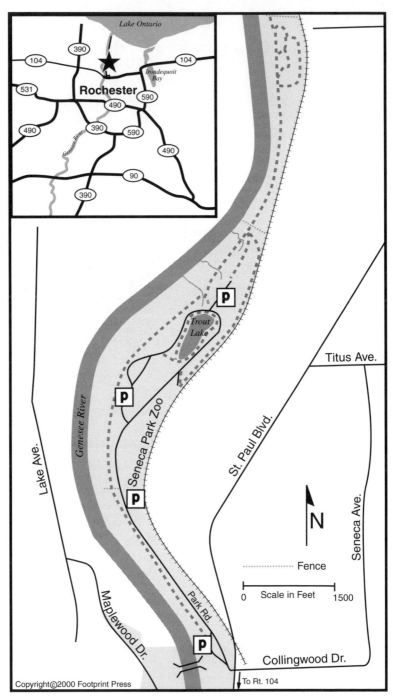

Seneca Park

22.

Seneca Park

Location:	Rochester, Monroe County
Directions:	From Route 104, exit north onto St. Paul Boulevard. Turn east onto Park Road toward the Seneca Park Zoo. Park at the first car turn around after entering the park, near the Monroe County Pure Waters bridge.
Length:	3 miles of trails
Difficulty:	Novice
Terrain:	Rolling hills
Trail Markings:	None
Uses:	Skiing, Snowshoeing, Hiking
Amenities:	None
Admission:	Free
Dogs:	OK on leash
Hours:	Dawn to dusk
Contact:	Monroe County Parks Department 171 Reservoir Avenue, Rochester, NY 14620 (716) 256-4950

For Snow Conditions Call: None

The 297-acre Seneca Park was designed by Frederick Law Olmsted who is considered to be the founder of landscape architecture. He was prolific in the Rochester area where he designed four major parks: Seneca, Genesee Valley, Highland, and Maplewood.

Olmsted's designs were revolutionary for the late 1800s. Instead of laying out precise squares and gardens, he planned clumps of woods, meandering trails, bridle paths and spectacular views. He planted trees carefully to effect a "forested" look. This natural, quiet look was half of Olmsted's design philosophy. The other half created spaces for more active use, such as the open areas for ball fields and ponds for swimming in summer and ice skating in winter. Pavilions and bridges were designed in a neo-classic style to separate activity areas.

> "A park should be accessible to the poor as well as the rich. It should be the beauty of the fields, the meadows, the prairies of green pastures, and the still waters. What we want to gain is tranquility and rest to the mind."
>
> Frederick Law Olmsted

In its days of grandeur, swan boats plied back and forth taking passengers for a ride on Trout Lake. The boats carried 15 to 20 passengers on bench seats while the driver sat on a cast iron seat between two 4 foot high swans and peddled the pontoon boat. Today a paved path and picnic tables encircle the lake. The park is also home to the Seneca Park Zoo.

Seneca Park continued:

The trail in Seneca Park runs parallel to the steep Genesee River gorge affording many spectacular views, especially with leaves off the trees. While there are no blazes, the trail is well defined and up to eight feet wide at times. Dock access trails lead left to the river's edge—these are too steep to ski.

The Monroe County Pure Waters bridge was built in 1988. The 670 foot pedestrian bridge gives an excellent view of the surrounding gorge and river 100 feet below. It connects to the Genesee River Trail on the west bank of the river. Unfortunately, this section of the Genesee River Trail follows sidewalks and gets plowed in winter.

Snowshoeing can be a leisurely walk or an invigorating romp.
Here, Reed Hoffmann demonstrates the aerobic variety.

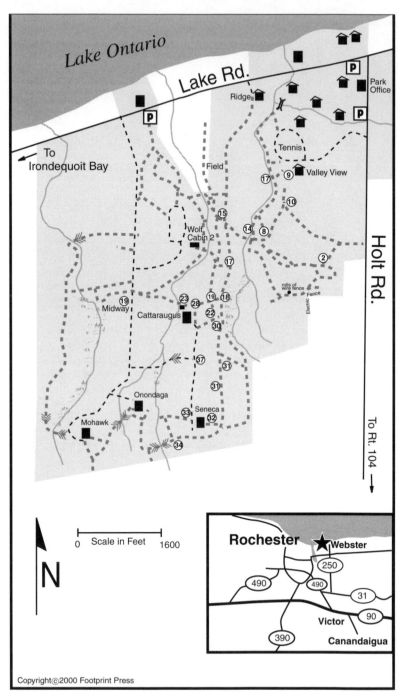

Webster Park

23.

Webster Park

Location:	Webster, Monroe County
Directions:	Lake Road parallels the Lake Ontario shore in Webster, east of Rochester. Two parking areas are available from Lake Road.
Length:	6 miles of trails
Difficulty:	Novice, Intermediate
Terrain:	Moderate Hills
Trail Markings:	Not fully marked, some blue-and-white and red-and-white numbered signs on posts at trail junctions, some ski markers
Uses:	Skiing, Snowshoeing, Hiking
Amenities:	Shelters
Admission:	Free
Dogs:	OK on leash
Hours:	Dawn to dusk
Contact:	Monroe County Parks Department 171 Reservoir Avenue, Rochester, NY 14620 (716) 256-4950

For Snow Conditions Call: None

Webster Park is heavily used by winter skiers. Its extensive network of intersecting trails means you can create many loops. The downside is that it's easy to get disoriented if you're not familiar with the area.

The only advanced area is the most southern section of the park, near Seneca, Onondaga, and Mohawk Lodges. The majority of trails are wide and easy for Novice skiers.

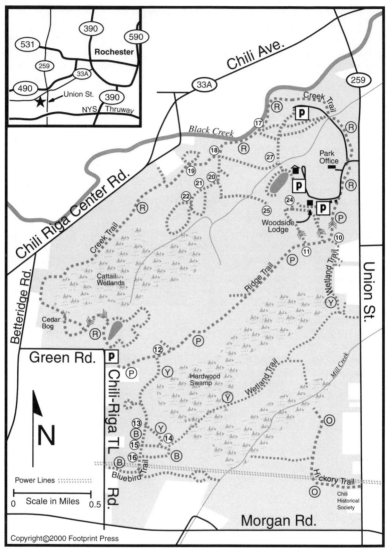

Black Creek Park

24.
Black Creek Park

Location:	Chili, Monroe County
Directions:	Take the Union Street exit off Interstate 490 and head south on Union Street. Turn right to enter Black Creek Park and follow the park road left to the parking area near Woodside Lodge.
Length:	10 miles of trails
Difficulty:	Novice, Intermediate
Terrain:	Rolling hills
Trail Markings:	Some junctions are marked with blue-and-white numbered signs on wooden posts, also colored arrow signs
Uses:	Skiing, Snowshoeing, Hiking
Amenities:	None
Admission:	Free
Dogs:	OK on leash
Hours:	7 AM - 11 PM
Contact:	Monroe County Parks Department 171 Reservoir Avenue, Rochester, NY 14620 (716) 256-4950

For Snow Conditions Call: None

Black Creek is the centerpiece of this park in southwestern Monroe County. Purchased in 1963, the park has large tracts of undeveloped, rolling hills with two small ponds. Its trails wind through tall brush and young forest areas. Six-foot wide paths are mowed throughout the park creating many possible snowshoeing or cross-country skiing loops. A recent addition of plastic floating bridges allowed the development of the Wetland Trail. Deer are plentiful in the park.

The historic Streeters Inn located on Union Street is now owned by the Monroe County Parks Department and is home to the Chili Historical Society. This inn was once a coach stop, tavern and inn and dates back to 1811. Call 256-4950 for more information.

Trail	Markings	Distance	Level of Difficulty
Ridge Trail	Purple	1.4 miles	Intermediate
Creek Trail	Red	3.1 miles	Intermediate
Hickory Trail	Orange	1.4 miles	Novice
Bluebird Trail	Blue	1.2 miles	Novice
Wetland Trail	Yellow	2.1 miles	Novice

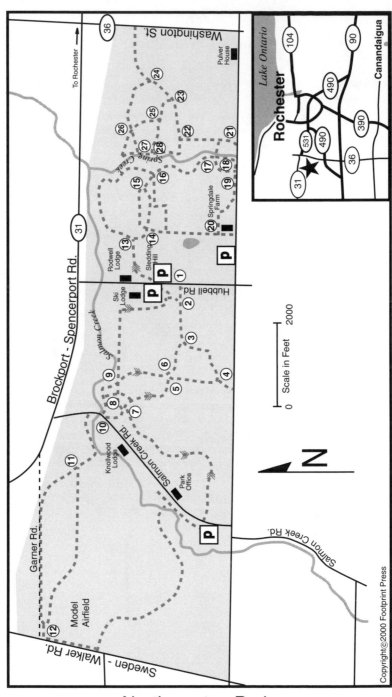

Northampton Park

25.

Northampton Park

Location:	Sweden & Ogden, Monroe County
Directions:	Take Route 31 west from Rochester. After passing Route 36, turn south on Hubbell Street or Salmon Creek Road to find the parking areas.
Length:	7.5 miles of trails
Difficulty:	Novice, Intermediate
Terrain:	Moderate Hills
Trail Markings:	Some blue-and-white numbered signs on posts at trail junctions, some ski markers
Uses:	Skiing, Snowshoeing, Hiking
Amenities:	Warming hut (ski lodge)
	Restrooms in ski lodge
Admission:	Free
Dogs:	OK on leash
Hours:	Dawn to dusk
Contact:	Monroe County Parks Department
	171 Reservoir Avenue, Rochester, NY 14620
	(716) 256-4950

For Snow Conditions Call: None

This 973 acre park, which straddles the Sweden-Ogden town line, combines a downhill ski slope and rope tow, a model airplane field, Salmon Creek, the Pulver House of the Ogden Historical Society, and Springdale Farm—a demonstration farm with chickens, peacocks, turkeys, horses, cows, goats, bunnies, pigs, lambs, and bulls. Originally, when the park was dedicated in 1964, it was named Salmon Creek Park. But, Northampton was later selected to honor the area's rich history and the former Township of Northampton.

The trails are predominantly 10-feet wide mowed swaths through tall bush, young trees, and meadows. Trails east of Hubbell Road and west of Salmon Creek Road are all easy, novice trails. Between Hubbell Road and Salmon Creek Road, the trails passing markers 3, 6, 9, and 8, and from 9 to the ski lodge are hillier intermediate trails.

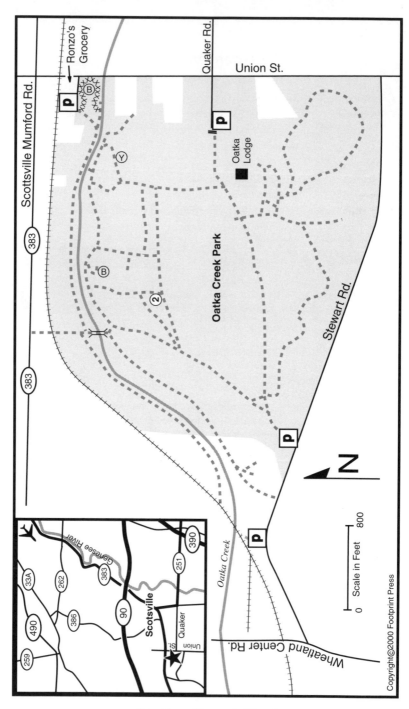

Oatka Creek Park

26.

Oatka Creek Park

Location:	Scottsville, Monroe County
Directions:	From Scottsville, head west on Route 383 (Scottsville Mumford Road). Turn south on Union Street and west into the parking area of Oatka Creek Park at the end of Quaker Road.
Length:	6 miles of trails
Difficulty:	Novice, Intermediate
Terrain:	Moderate hills
Trail Markings:	None
Uses:	Skiing, Snowshoeing, Hiking
Amenities:	None
Admission:	Free
Dogs:	OK on leash
Hours:	Dawn to dusk
Contact:	Monroe County Parks Department 171 Reservoir Avenue, Rochester, NY 14620 (716) 256-4950

For Snow Conditions Call: None

Under this lush, wooded park lies a soft-gray colored rock called gypsum. Gypsum was used by early farmers as fertilizer, later becoming this country's first cement. Today it is used in wallboard for home construction. 150 years ago, workers hauled it to the surface with ropes, loaded it into small carts, and pulled it by mules to a mill nearby. Chemically, gypsum is calcium sulfate and gradually turns soil sour (or acidic). Because dogwood, azalea, and mosses prefer this type of soil, these types of vegetation abound in Oatka Creek Park. Oatka Creek Park is best known for brown trout fishing in Oatka Creek when snow doesn't cover the ground.

The terrain is gentle but some of the trails are narrow. This is the place to come for quiet solitude away from the maddening crowds. Novices should stay in the southern section of the park. The trails north of Oatka Creek are especially narrow. The Blue Trail south of Ronzo's Grocery winds through old stone ruins and is fun to explore when there's no snow, but sections are too steep for skiing.

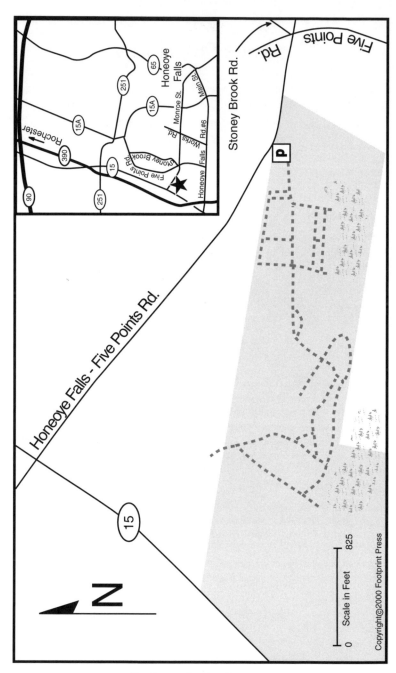

Quinn Oak Openings

27.

Quinn Oak Openings

Location:	Rush, Monroe County
Directions:	From Route 15 (south of Rochester), turn east on Honeoye Falls-Five Points Road. Watch for the Quinn Oak Openings parking area on the south side of Honeoye Falls-Five Points Road.
Length:	3.1 miles of trails
Difficulty:	Intermediate
Terrain:	Mostly flat, some moderate hills
Trail Markings:	None
Uses:	Skiing, Snowshoeing, Hiking
Amenities:	None
Admission:	Free
Dogs:	OK
Hours:	Dawn to dusk
Contact:	NYS Department of Environmental Conservation–Forestry 7291 Coon Road, Bath, NY 14810 (607) 776-2165 ext. 10 http://www.dec.state.ny.us

For Snow Conditions Call: None

The sign at the parking area reads "Quinn Oak Openings–Area of Exceptional Forest Character." This wonderfully diverse area is a magical place for us humans to wander in winter.

Approximately 4,000 years ago a major drought caused the demise of many native species of trees and allowed midwestern prairie plants to move east. It created fields of tall grass prairies surrounded by oak forests–an oak opening. The Indians noticed that these grass openings were havens from bugs and allowed them to get a broader view of approaching enemies so they kept the grasslands open with fire. The absence of trees in the oak openings made them easy targets for farmers. As white settlers moved in, many of the oak openings were put to use to raise crops.

Quinn Oak Openings is one of fewer than 20 oak openings remaining in the world. It was spared because limestone is only a few inches below the surface. This land was privately owned and was used to graze cows. The farmers continued periodic burnings to encourage grass growth. Today, DEC continues this practice to save this unique resource.

Sometimes the DEC mows new channels through the grasslands, so the trails shown on the map may vary. Even so, this area is worth exploration. It's unlikely that you'll run into other humans. You're more likely to scare up the resident deer.

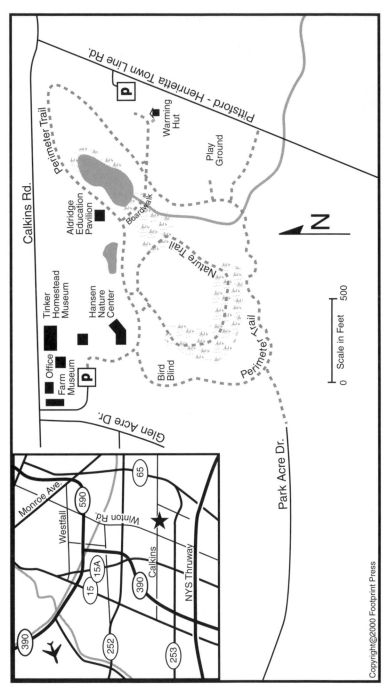

Tinker Nature Park

28.

Tinker Nature Park

Location:	Henrietta, Monroe County
Directions:	Exit I-390 at Hylan Drive and head south. At the end, turn left onto Calkins Road. Tinker Nature Park will be on the right.
Length:	2.5 miles of trails
Difficulty:	Novice
Terrain:	Flat
Trail Markings:	Some wooden signs
Uses:	Skiing, Snowshoeing, Hiking
Amenities:	Warming hut and nature center
	Restrooms (in nature center)
	Snowshoe rentals ($2/day)
Admission:	Free
Dogs:	Pets NOT allowed
Hours:	Dawn to dusk
Contact:	Tinker Nature Park
	1525 Calkins Road, Pittsford, NY 14534
	(716) 359-7044

For Snow Conditions Call: (716) 359-7044

The land for Tinker Nature Park was donated by the Aldridge family in 1991 and made public in 1994. The well designed park has become a year-round favorite for people of all ages. It consists of woods, wetland, ponds, and fields which together create a living museum of natural history. Within the park is the Hansen Nature Center, offering classes in cross-country skiing, snowshoeing, photography, wild flowers, song birds, etc. The nature center building is open Tuesday through Saturday, 9 AM to 3 PM, and Sundays 11 AM to 3 PM.

Trail	Distance	Level of Difficulty
Perimeter Trail	1.2 mile loop	Novice
Nature Trail	0.5 mile loop	Novice

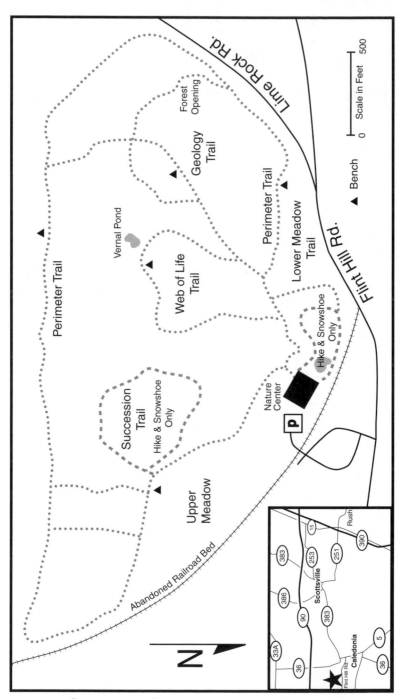

Genesee Country Nature Center

29.

Genesee Country Nature Center

Location: Mumford, Monroe County

Directions: From Route 36, turn west onto Flint Hill Road just north of Caledonia. Turn left into Genesee Country Museum and follow the signs to the nature center parking area.

Length: 4.5 miles of ski trails

1.4 miles of snowshoe trails

Difficulty: Novice, Intermediate

Terrain: Mostly flat, some moderate hills

Trail Markings: Wooden trail signs at junctions

Uses: Skiing, Snowshoeing, Hiking

Amenities: Warming hut (nature center)

Restrooms (in nature center)

Groomed and set-tracked trails

Ski ($8/day) and snowshoe ($3/day) rentals

Admission: Adults $2.50, Seniors $2, Children 4-16 $1.50

Dogs: Pets NOT allowed

Hours: 10 AM-4 PM Thursday - Friday, 10 AM-5 PM weekends

Contact: Genesee Country Nature Center
1410 Flint Hill Road, PO Box 310, Mumford, NY 14511
www.gcv.org
(716) 538-6822

For Snow Conditions Call: (716) 538-6822, ext 262

Genesee Country Nature Center is part of Genesee Country Museum, a reconstructed community from the 1800s with 57 restored and fully furnished buildings. The nature center has a classroom building with nature exhibits and nearly five miles of trails. Special events are held throughout the year.

The trails within Genesee Country Nature Center are mostly flat with a few rolling hills making this an ideal place for a family adventure. The land was once farmed and now contains a mixture of fields and young forests.

Trail	Marking	Distance	Use
Perimeter Trail	Yellow	2.25 miles	Skiing
Geology Trail	Green	1.5 miles	Skiing
Web of Life Trail	Blue	0.8 mile	Skiing
Lower Meadow Trail	Black	0.3 mile	Snowshoeing
Succession Trail	Orange	1.1 miles	Snowshoeing

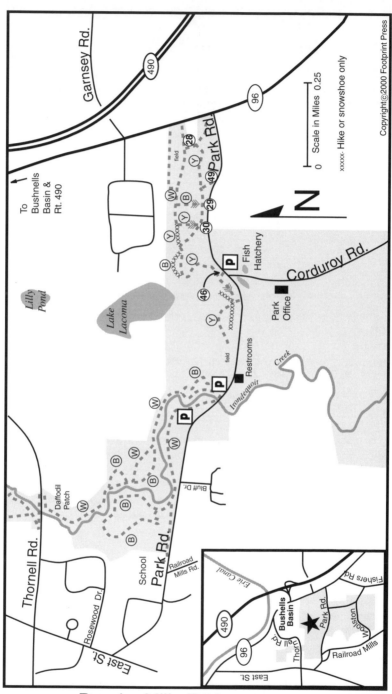

Powder Mills Park (North Section)

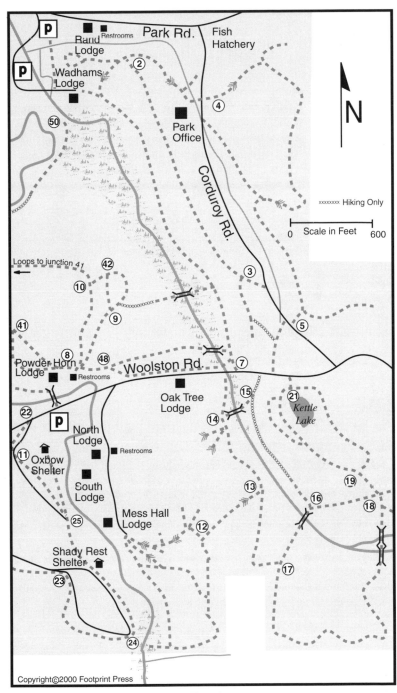

Powder Mills Park (South Section)

30.
Powder Mills Park

Location:	Bushnells Basin, Monroe County
Directions:	From Route 96 south of Bushnells Basin, turn west on Park Road. The parking area for the north section is on the east side of Irondequoit Creek where the creek flows under Park Road. For the south section, turn south off Park Road onto Corduroy Road, then west on Woolston Road. The parking area is before Oak Tree Lodge.
Length:	8 miles of trails
Difficulty:	Novice, Intermediate, Advanced
Terrain:	Hilly
Trail Markings:	Some trails are blazed, some have blue numbered signs at intersections.
Uses:	Skiing, Snowshoeing, Hiking
Amenities:	Shelters
Admission:	Free
Dogs:	OK on leash
Hours:	6 AM - 11 PM
Contact:	Monroe County Parks Department 171 Reservoir Avenue, Rochester, NY 14620 (716) 256-4950

For Snow Conditions Call: None

Set in steep, wooded hills, Powder Mills Park offers downhill skiing as well as a network of trails for all abilities of cross-country skiing.

Development of the area began in 1850 when Daniel C. Rand arrived from Middletown, CT, where he worked as a manufacturer of blasting powder. Rand came to this area and chose a small, ideal spot, far enough from settlements, but still close to the Erie Canal. In 1852 Rand opened his mill for making blasting powder in partnership with Mortimer Wadhams, and called it the Rand & Wadhams Powder Company.

The process for making blasting powder, which is simply a course version of gun powder, had been known for 100 years and involves grinding and mixing saltpeter (potassium nitrate), sulfur, and charcoal. To be an effective explosive, the ingredients have to be ground to an extremely fine consistency.

Irondequoit Creek was dammed to create a pond and a millrace for power to turn the great grinding stones and other machines used to pulverize the ingredients of blasting power. But it was a dangerous job. While in Connecticut, Rand had witnessed several accidents and his attention was drawn to the Rochester area by news of explosions that destroyed some powder mills in Allens Creek.

During construction of his new mill, Rand took several measures to help prevent or lessen the consequences of possible explosions. First each step of the process was performed in a separate building so an explosion in one would not send the whole business up in flames.

Rand also sought to eliminate sparks caused by metal touching metal. The buildings were connected by a narrow-gage railroad with wooden rails on which rode small cars with wooden wheels. Employees were not allowed to have any metal in their clothing. Many men even wore felt-soled slippers because their regular boots were constructed with nails.

Finally, to lessen the chance of fires or vandalism, Rand kept the property off limits to all hunting, fishing, and camping. This created the air of mystery about the area that lingered years after the mills were gone. In the 58 years of operation, several small explosions and two injuries occurred at the mill, but no catastrophic explosions or deaths.

Rand bought saltpeter and sulfur, but made his own charcoal out of willow trees that grew abundantly in the valley. Over the years Rand planted hundreds of new willows to replace those he cut. The willow was burned very slowly to produce charcoal. The charcoal and sulfur were ground together, with the saltpeter being ground separately. After both were reduced to course grain, they were combined and ground together for several hours. They were then formed into large cakes under 3,000 to 4,000 pounds pressure. The cakes in turn were re-ground with graphite, which made the powder flow better. The powder was then sieved to different grades and packed in 25-pound kegs, with the finest being the most powerful blasting powder.

Rand died in 1883 and his partner passed on 3 years later. Rand's two sons, Mortimer and Samuel, continued the mill operation under the name D.C. Rand Powder Co. The brothers quit the business in 1910 and moved to Uniontown, PA, to set up another mill closer to the coal mines that consumed the powder.

The property and buildings were left vacant until 1929 when 290 acres were purchased by the Monroe County Parks Commission. At that time the mill and homestead were razed.

Two maps are provided to show both north and south section trails. For novice skiing use the area north of Woolston Road identified by markers 7, 48, 8, 41, 10, 42, 9 and marker 9 north past Wadhams Lodge to Park Road. Also, the trails parallel to Irondequoit Creek north of Park Road.

For intermediate skiing use the area south of Woolston Road identified by markers 14, 13, 12, 17, 16, 18, 19, and 21.

Advanced skiers can head east of Corduroy Road from marker 4 to 5 and north of Park Road between Irondequoit Creek and Route 96, passing markers 46, 30, 29, and 28.

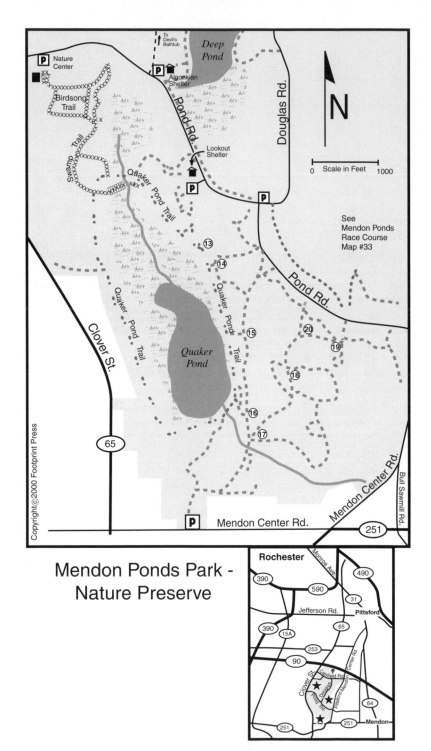

Mendon Ponds Park - Nature Preserve

31.

Mendon Ponds Park
Nature Preserve

Location:	Mendon, Monroe County
Directions:	From Route 65 (Clover Street) head east on Pond Road. For snowshoeing, park at the nature center. For skiing, park at he Lookout Shelter parking area.
Length:	2 miles of snowshoe trails
	7 miles of ski trails
Difficulty:	Novice
Terrain:	Flat & rolling hills
Trail Markings:	Some blue-and-white numbered signs on posts at trail junctions, some ski markers
Uses:	Skiing, Snowshoeing, Hiking
Amenities:	Warming hut (nature center)
	Heated restrooms at nature center
	Outhouse at Lookout Shelter
	Groomed trails (sporadically)
	Shelter
	Snowshoe rentals: $2/day, Thurs.-Sun., 11 AM-3 PM
Admission:	Free
Dogs:	Pets NOT allowed
Hours:	Dawn to dusk
Contact:	Monroe County Parks Department
	171 Reservoir Avenue, Rochester, NY 14620
	(716) 256-4950

For Snow Conditions Call: (716) 334-3780

This is a jewel in Monroe County's park system, filled with lakes, woods, and rolling hills. The Mendon Ponds Nature Center offers weekly family programs and is open Thursday through Sunday from 11 AM until 4 PM. Stop by to rent snowshoes and see the exhibits. They also provide a schedule of events, or call (716) 334-3780. From the nature center you can snowshoe on the 1.1-mile Birdsong Trail loop and the 0.8-mile Swamp Trail loop.

The network of easy ski trails leave from the Lookout Shelter parking area. You can circle Quaker Pond for a 2.5-mile loop or explore the rolling hills of the mowed grassland area east of Quaker Pond. All trails are wide and easy to follow.

Don't be surprised if black-capped chickadees fly near you and even try to land on your head or shoulders. These friendly critters are accustomed to being fed year-round by people enjoying the trails. Take a few sunflower seeds with you and the birds will land on your outstretched hand to get the goodies.

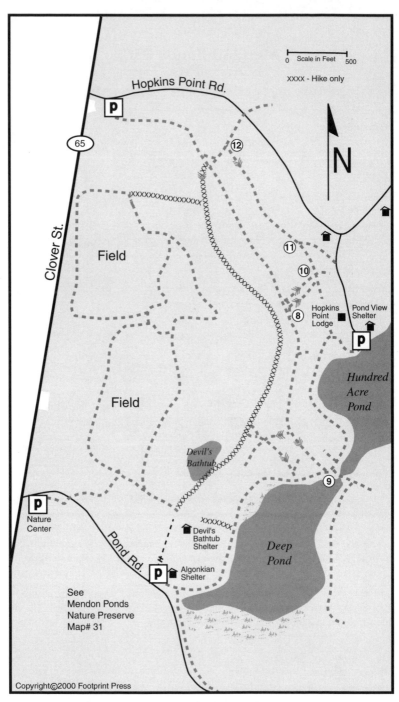

Mendon Ponds Park - Glacial Area

32.

Mendon Ponds Park
Glacial Area

Location:	Mendon, Monroe County
Directions:	From Route 65 (Clover Street) head east on Pond Road. Park at the Algonkian Shelter parking area.
Length:	4.5 miles of trails
Difficulty:	Novice - trails near the ponds and around the fields
	Advanced - the eskers northwest of Devil's Bathtub
Terrain:	Flat near ponds, otherwise hilly
Trail Markings:	Some blue-and-white numbered signs on posts at trail junctions, some ski markers
Uses:	Skiing, Snowshoeing, Hiking
Amenities:	Heated restrooms at nature center, Hopkins Point and beach area
	Shelters
	Snowshoe rentals at nature center
Admission:	Free
Dogs:	OK on leash
Hours:	Dawn to dusk
Contact:	Monroe County Parks Department
	171 Reservoir Avenue, Rochester, NY 14620
	(716) 256-4950

For Snow Conditions Call: None

Mendon Ponds Park was named a National Natural Landmark because of its unique glacial land forms. Its geologic features were formed by the last of four major glaciers that covered the area 12,000 to 14,000 years ago. The glacier reached to the Pennsylvania border and was 5,000 to 10,000 feet thick. As the ice melted, large amounts of sand, rock, and gravel were deposited. Three main geologic features visible in the park today are: kames, eskers, and kettles (see definitions on page 222.)

People from all over the country come to study "Devil's Bathtub." This kettle is a rare meromictic lake, of which there are only a few in the world. A meromictic lake is a very deep body of water surrounded by high ridges. Because the high ridges prevent the wind from blowing on the water, the lake's water levels never turn over and the motionless surface gives the lake a mirrored effect.

This segment of the park includes trails that climb to the tops of kames and eskers resulting in challenging terrain. To avoid the steep sections, stay on the trails parallel to ponds or to the western section where the trails circumnavigate large fields.

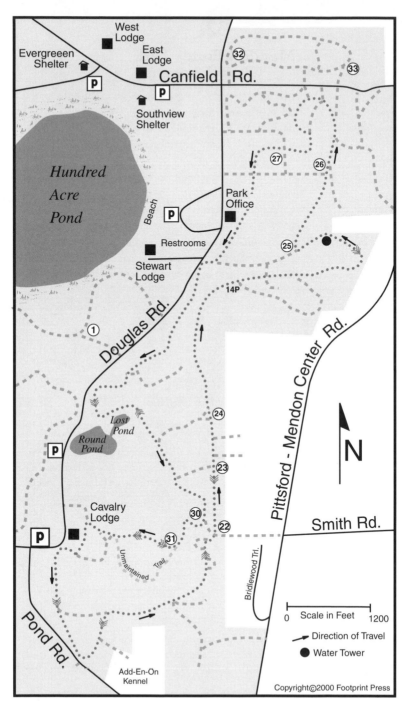

Mendon Ponds Park - Race Course

33.
Mendon Ponds Park
Race Course

Location:	Mendon, Monroe County
Directions:	From Route 65 (Clover Street) head east on Canfield Road then south on Douglas Road. Park at either the beach parking lot or the lot at the intersection with Pond Road.
Length:	8 miles of trails
	The outer loop (groomed trail) is 5.7 miles around
Difficulty:	Intermediate, Advanced
Terrain:	Hilly
Trail Markings:	Some blue-and-white numbered signs on posts at trail junctions, some ski markers
Uses:	Skiing, Hiking
Amenities:	Heated restrooms at beach parking area
	Groomed trails
Admission:	Free
Dogs:	OK on leash
Hours:	Dawn to dusk
Contact:	Monroe County Parks Department
	171 Reservoir Avenue, Rochester, NY 14620
	(716) 256-4950

For Snow Conditions Call: None

Mendon Ponds Park is the largest park in Monroe County. The first inhabitants of this area were the Algonquin, Iroquois, and Seneca Indians who left behind many Indian trails. On July 23, 1687, the Marquis de Denonville's army used the trails to attack the Indians in the region. In his memoirs, Denonville recalls looking down from the top of one of the ridges at "three pretty little lakes," the first reference to Mendon Ponds in our recorded history. The first white settler in the Mendon Ponds area was Joshua Lillie, who is buried on a small plot on Wilmarth Road. The park was dedicated in 1928 and now has 30 miles of winding trails.

It is a busy place year-round. In winter the race course area of trails are groomed. Local schools use these trails for cross-country ski races. To insure safety of all skiers, the trails are marked for one-way traffic. The area south of the park office is quite hilly. For easier trails, stick to the northern section and the flat trail through a pine woods north of Canfield Road (markers 32 and 33).

No one has discovered two snowflakes with exactly the same crystal pattern.

However, most snowflakes are based on a hexagon — a six-way star symmetry. Each snowflake reflects the topsy-turvy path it takes through the air from creation in the wintry sky to its final resting place on the ground. It grows six unique arms during its flight.

Livingston, Ontario & Yates Counties

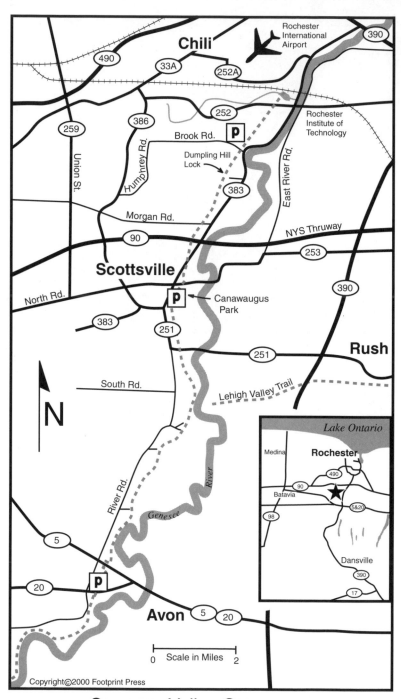

Genesee Valley Greenway
Scottsville to Avon (North Section)

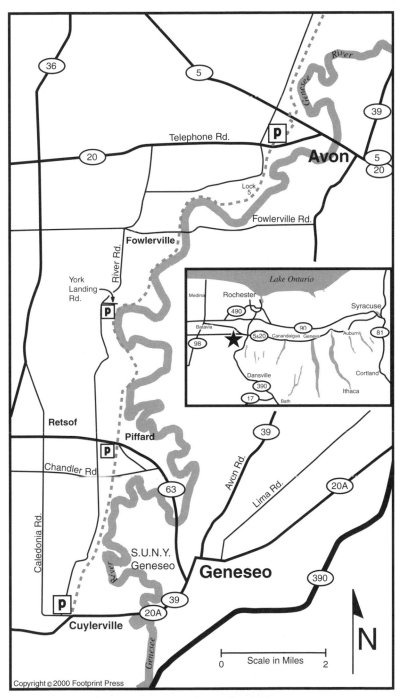

Genesee Valley Greeenway
Avon to Cuylerville (South Section)

34.

Genesee Valley Greenway
Scottsville to Cuylerville

Location:	Monroe & Livingston Counties
Directions:	See various parking areas shown on the maps
Length:	25 miles one way
Difficulty:	Novice (road crossings required)
Terrain:	Flat to mild hills
Trail Markings:	White, metal "Genesee Valley Greenway" signs and yellow, metal gates at road crossings
Uses:	Skiing, Snowshoeing, Hiking, Snowmobiling
Amenities:	None (restaurants available in Scottsville)
Admission:	Free
Dogs:	OK on leash
Hours:	6 AM - 10 PM
Contacts:	Friends of the Genesee Valley Greenway, Inc.
	P.O. Box 42, Mount Morris, NY 14510
	(716) 658-2569, email fogvg@aol.com
	http://www.netacc.net/~fogvg
	Regional Land Manager
	NYS Department of Environmental Conservation
	7291 Coon Road, Bath, NY 14810
	(607) 776-2165
	http://www.dec.state.ny.us

For Snow Conditions Call: None

The Genesee Valley Greenway will be a 90-mile multi-use trail which follows a transportation route that was used by the Genesee Valley Canal, from 1840 to 1878, and by the railroad, from 1880 to the mid 1960s. Currently, 47 miles of the total 90 miles are open for use. It is a work-in-progress. Each year more mileage is opened and segments are connected.

This segment of the Genesee Valley Greenway passes through wetlands, woodlands, rolling farmlands, and the Genesee River valley. Don't expect a boring railroad bed—it winds to follow the Genesee River. Along the way you'll find remains of Dumpling Hill Lock and Lock 5. Watch for lone oak trees in the farm fields. Land leases in the 1700s required the preservation of one large shade tree every 2 acres. Many of these trees are over 200 years old.

Distance between parking areas:

Brook Road to Canawaugus Park	4.6 miles
Canawaugus Park to Route 20	8.4 miles
Route 20 to York Landing Road	5.9 miles
York Landing Road to Route 63	2.9 miles
Route 63 to Route 20A	3.8 miles

Victor and Jennifer Perotti make skiing look easy.

On average, it takes 10 inches of snow to melt down to approximately one inch of liquid rain.

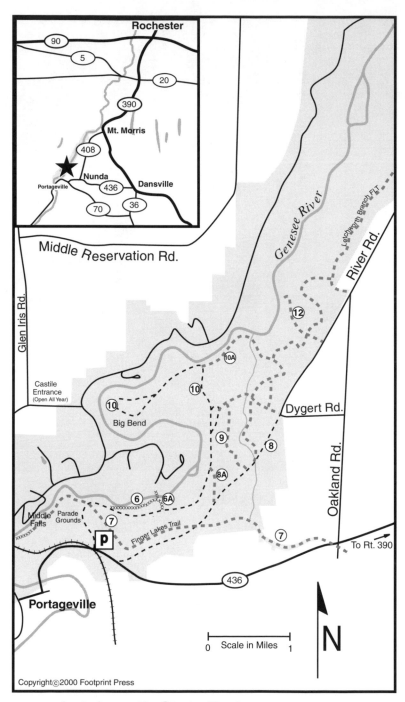

Letchworth State Park (East of Genesee River)

35.

Letchworth State Park
East of the Genesee River

Location:	Portageville, Livingston County
Directions:	Follow Route 436 at the south end of Letchworth State Park, between Nunda and Portageville. Park at the Parade Grounds area. This entrance is closed in winter but there is room for cars before the gate. Do not block the gates (emergency vehicle access).
Length:	18 miles of trails and unplowed roads
Difficulty:	Novice, Intermediate
Terrain:	Flat, gentle slopes
Trail Markings:	Some signs, some blazes
Uses:	Skiing, Snowshoeing, Hiking
Amenities:	None (trails open to snowmobiles are sometimes groomed)
Admission:	Free
Dogs:	OK on leash
Hours:	Dawn to dusk
Contact:	Letchworth State Park, NYSOPRHP, Genesee Region 1 Letchworth State Park, Castile, NY 14427-1124 (716) 493-3600

For Snow Conditions Call: (716) 493-3600

The Parade Grounds was an infantry parade grounds during the Civil War. The unplowed park road heads first downhill, then gradually uphill to a network of trails on the plateau above the Genesee River valley. Bear left to Big Bend for views of the gorge cliffs where they're the highest. At Big Bend, the Genesee River almost doubles over on itself. This twisting is unusual for such deep canyons. In its early days, more than 10,000 years ago, the Genesee River crossed a plateau. It was free to sidewind like a snake as it began to cut through the sandstone and shale. Once the winding course was set, the river dug its way down to create the 600-foot cliffs of today. Loop back on any of the other trails which are a combination of dirt roads and woods trails.

Trail	Distance	Level of Difficulty	Snowmobiles
Unplowed Road	3.0 miles	Novice	Yes
6 (Portage)	0.5 mile	Hike/snowshoe only	No
6A (Foot Bridge)	0.5 mile	Hike/snowshoe only	No
7 (Genesee Valley)	5.8 miles	Novice	Yes
8 (River Road)	2.8 miles	Novice	Yes
8A (Blue Jay Road)	0.5 mile	Intermediate	Yes
9 (Dishmill Creek)	3.0 miles	Intermediate	No
10 (Big Bend Road)	2.5 miles	Novice	Yes
10A (Trillium)	0.5 mile	Novice	No

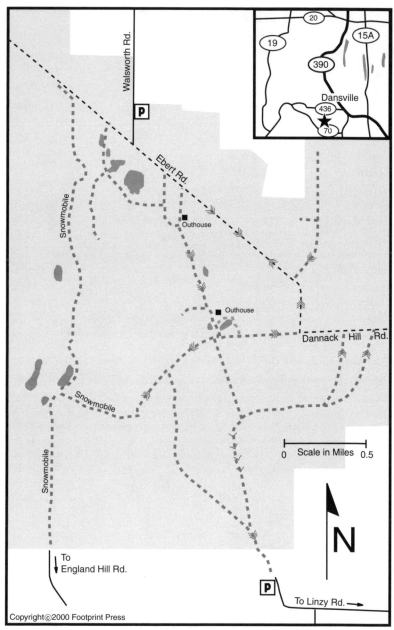

Rattlesnake Hill

36.

Rattlesnake Hill

Location:	West of Dansville, Livingston and Allegany Counties
Directions:	From Dansville, head west on Route 436. Turn south onto Shute Road, then south again on Walsworth Road. Parking is at the end of Walsworth Road.
Length:	10 miles of trails
Difficulty:	Novice, Intermediate
Terrain:	Hilly
Trail Markings:	None
Uses:	Skiing, Snowshoeing, Hiking, Snowmobiling
Amenities:	None
Admission:	Free
Dogs:	OK on leash
Hours:	Dawn to dusk
Contact:	Regional Wildlife Manager NYS Department of Environmental Conservation 6274 East Avon-Lima Road, Avon, New York 14414 (716) 226-2466 http://www.dec.state.ny.us

For Snow Conditions Call: None

Rattlesnake Hill Wildlife Management Area is a 5,100-acre tract of high elevation land. The plateau has gentle rolling hills on the summit but has steep sides. Due to the elevation, it gets snow when lower areas are bare.

The land was purchased in the 1930s under the Federal Resettlement Administration when the depletion of the farmland made farming the area unprofitable. The area was turned over to the DEC to be managed as a wildlife habitat. Don't let the name of this area scare you away, rattlesnakes (if there were any left in the area) hibernate in winter.

As a wildlife management area, Rattlesnake Hill is open to hunting, so be sure to wear bright colors if you venture out during hunting season. The animals found here include white-tailed deer, wild turkey, ruffed grouse, gray squirrel, cottontail rabbit, snowshoe hare, mink, beaver, and raccoon. Winter is a great time to spot the wildlife at Rattlesnake Hill.

Ebert Road is part of your winter trail. It's a seasonal road that is closed to cars from November 15 to April 1. A few of the trails are used by snowmobiles (as marked on the map). This means the trails may be hard packed for easy skiing or you may compete with speeding machines, depending on your timing. You can avoid the snowmobiles by staying on the other trails.

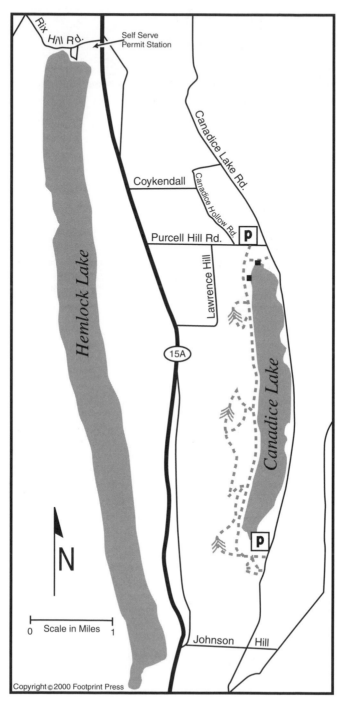

Canadice Lake Trail

37.
Canadice Lake Trail

Location:	West side of Canadice Lake, Ontario County
Directions:	From Route 15A, head east on Purcell Hill Road at the north end of Canadice Lake. The parking area is east of Canadice Hollow Road.
Length:	6 miles of trails
Difficulty:	Novice, Advanced
Terrain:	Flat along the lake, steep hills on side loop trails
Trail Markings:	12 x 18-inch, green-and-white signs labeled with hiker silhouettes and "Hemlock Canadice Watershed"
Uses:	Skiing, Snowshoeing, Hiking
Amenities:	None
Admission:	Free, but a Watershed Visitor Permit is required. Pick one up at the permit station on Rix Hill Road or get it online at www.ci.rochester.ny.us/watershedpermit.htm
Dogs:	OK on leash
Hours:	Dawn to dusk
Contact:	City of Rochester, Water and Lighting Bureau 7412 Rix Hill Road, Hemlock, NY 14466 (716) 346-2617

For Snow Conditions Call: None

Long ago, Canadice Lake had cottages all along its shore. In 1872, the city of Rochester decided to use Canadice and Hemlock Lakes as a water supply. The first conduit for water was completed in 1876. By 1947, Rochester purchased all of the shoreline property and removed the cottages so that it could protect the water supply for its growing population. Although it was difficult for the cottage residents to leave their land, this area is now free of the commercialization that is so rampant on the other Finger Lakes. Ninety-foot-deep Canadice Lake is the smallest of the Finger Lakes, but it has the highest elevation, at 1,096 feet. This makes it a good water supply for the city and a good source of snowy trails for winter outdoor enthusiasts.

To protect city property and the supply of drinking water, the city requires all visitors to obtain a Watershed Visitor Permit, one of the easiest permits to obtain. Just stop at the visitor's self-serve, permit station located at the north end of Hemlock Lake on Rix Hill Road off Route 15A. There are no fees or forms to fill out, but the permit document details the dos and don'ts to help keep the area pristine, so it's important to read it.

The 3.7 mile long trail that parallels the lake is flat for easy skiing. For a challenge, head west, on the trails that wind up the hillside. You'll find some short, steep sections.

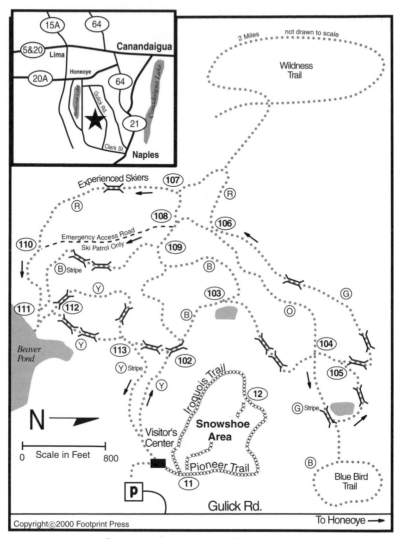

Cumming Nature Center

38.

Cumming Nature Center

Location:	West of Canandaigua Lake, Ontario County
Directions:	From Route 20A in Honeoye, follow County Road 33 south to Pinewood Hill Road, then turn south on Gulick Road. From Naples, take Clark Street west to Gulick Road north.
Length:	15 miles of skiable trails
	2 miles reserved exclusively for snowshoeing
Difficulty:	Novice, Intermediate, Advanced
Terrain:	Some flat, some hills
Trail Markings:	Numbered signs at trail junctions
Uses:	Skiing, Snowshoeing
Amenities:	Warming Hut
	Restrooms
	Ski ($10/day) & snowshoe ($3/day) rentals
	Groomed & set-tracked trails
Admission:	$4
Dogs:	Pets NOT allowed
Hours:	Wednesday through Sunday, 9 AM-4:30 PM
Contact:	Rochester Museum & Science Center
	Cumming Nature Center
	6472 Gulick Road, Naples, NY 14512
	www.rmsc.org
	(716) 374-6160

For Snow Conditions Call: (716) 374-6160

Cumming Nature Center is a 900-acre environmental education center and living museum operated by the Rochester Museum & Science Center. It contains a visitor center, beaver pond, a log cabin, a sugarhouse, oxen, and lots of trails. The center is active year-round with various fun and educational activities and festivals.

The first week after Christmas, the center opens for cross-country skiing on a network of trails that is even more extensive than the hiking trails open the rest of the year. The ski trails are patrolled by the Genesee Valley Nordic Ski Patrol.

The 0.6-mile Iroquois Trail and 0.75-mile Pioneer Trail are reserved for snowshoeing. The remaining 15 miles of trails are groomed and set-tracked for skiing. The one exception is the downhill section of Trail 5 (red) which is groomed but not set-tracked. See the table on the next page for specifics on each trail.

Cumming Nature Center trails continued:

Trail	Marking	Distance	Difficulty Level
Trail 1	Yellow	1.5 mile loop	Novice
Trail 2	Blue	0.75 mile loop	Novice
Trail 3	Blue stripe	0.75 mile	Intermediate
Trail 5	Red	1.0 mile	Intermediate
Wilderness Trail	Black & yellow stripe	2.0 mile loop	Advanced
Trail 6	Orange	1.5 miles	Intermediate
Trail 7	Green	1.0 mile	Intermediate
Trail 8	Green stripe	0.75 mile loop	Intermediate
Trail 9	Yellow stripe	0.25 mile	Novice
Blue Bird Trail	Blue polk-a-dot	0.75 mile loop	Intermediate
Iroquois Trail	Pink & black stripe	0.6 mile loop	Snowshoe only
Pioneer Trail	Pink & black stripe	0.75 mile loop	Snowshoe only

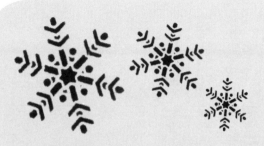

Does it have to be 32°F or colder for it to snow?

It has been known to snow with temperatures in the mid-40s °F. Temperatures are below 32°F up in the clouds where the snow is forming.

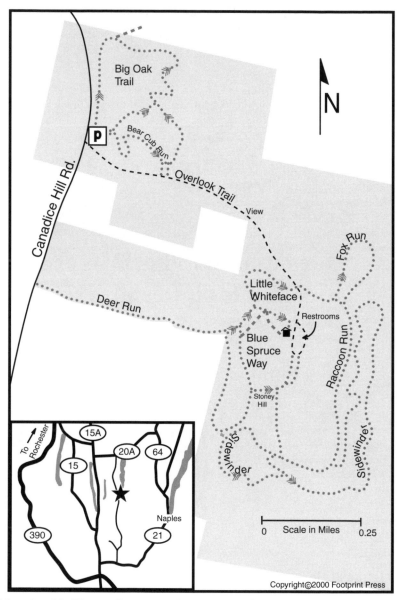

Harriet Hollister Spencer Memorial State Recreation Area

39.
Harriet Hollister Spencer
Memorial State Recreation Area

Location:	South of Honeoye Lake, Ontario County
Directions:	From Route 390, head east on Route 20A through Livonia. Continue east past Route 15A. Turn south on Canadice Hill Road. Pass Ross Road. Canadice Hill Road will turn to gravel. Turn left at the sign "Harriet Hollister Spencer Memorial Recreation Area." The parking area is on the left near the park entrance.
Length:	16 miles of trails
Difficulty:	Novice, Intermediate, Advanced
Terrain:	Varied
Trail Markings:	Numbered signs at trail junctions
Uses:	Skiing, Snowshoeing, Hiking,
Amenities:	Shelter
	Restrooms
	Groomed
Admission:	Free
Dogs:	OK on leash
Hours:	Dawn to dusk
Contact:	NYS Office of Parks, Recreation and Historic Preservation Stony Brook State Park 10820 Route 36 South, Dansville, NY 14437 (716) 335-8111

For Snow Conditions Call: None

High in the hills, between Canadice Lake and Honeoye Lake, this woodland area is treasured by winter enthusiasts because it often has snow when the surrounding area doesn't. The trails in this park are constructed, maintained, and groomed in winter by volunteers from the NYS Section 5 Ski League. Throughout winter you're likely to run into school ski teams practicing or racing on these trails. It's a popular area for all levels.

In summer you can drive the 1.5 miles into the shelter area. In winter this unplowed road becomes part of the ski network. It affords a view of Honeoye Lake in the valley to the north.

Trail	Distance	Difficulty Level
Overlook Trail	1.5 miles	Novice
Big Oak/Bear Cub Trails	1.9 mile loop	Intermediate
Raccoon Run	0.6 mile	Novice
Fox Run	0.6 mile	Advanced
Sidewinder Trail	1.5 miles	Advanced
Blue Spruce Way	1.5 miles	Advanced
Deer Run	0.5 mile	Advanced

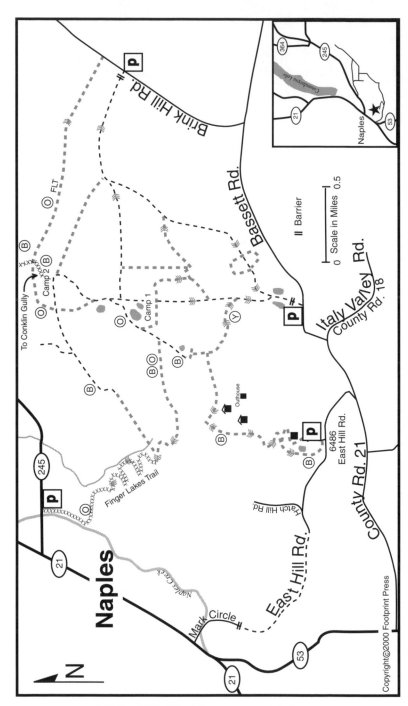

Hi Tor Wildlife Management Area

40.

Hi Tor Wildlife Management Area

Location:	Naples, Ontario & Yates Counties
Directions:	From Route 21 (Main St., Naples) heading south, bear left (S) on Route 53. Turn east onto County Road 21 (toward Italy Valley) then left onto Bassett Road.The parking area will be on the left. Brink and Bassett Road parking areas may not be plowed.
Length:	16 miles of trails and old logging roads
Difficulty:	Intermediate, Advanced
Terrain:	Hilly
Trail Markings:	Orange blazes on the Bristol Hills Branch of the Finger Lakes Trail, blue blazes on side trails, round, yellow plastic markers on some trails
Uses:	Skiing, Snowshoeing, Hiking
Amenities:	Shelters, winter camping near the shelters only
	Outhouse near the shelters
Admission:	Free
Dogs:	OK on leash
Hours:	Dawn to dusk
Contacts:	Regional Wildlife Manager
	NYS Department of Environmental Conservation
	6274 East Avon-Lima Road, Avon, New York 14414
	(716) 226-2466
	www.dec.state.ny.us
	Finger Lakes Trail Conference
	PO Box 18048, Rochester, NY 14618-0048
	(716) 288-7191
	www. fingerlakes.net/ trailsystem
	George Fraley, Fire Warden 28
	6486 East Hill Road, Naples, NY 14512
	(716) 374-5241

For Snow Conditions Call: None

Hi Tor (sometimes spelled High Tor) is an old English word meaning high, craggy hill or peak. You'll agree with the "high" part as you climb steeply up East Hill. The crags are the sharp gullies and eroded cliffs which cross this hill, making it scenic and physically challenging.

The Bristol Hills Branch of the Finger Lakes Trail (orange-blazed) traverses Hi Tor Wildlife Management Area. This is a spur trail, which runs for 54 miles from Ontario County Park in the north until it meets the main Finger Lakes Trail at Mitchellsville (near the southern end of Keuka Lake). The Bristol Hills Branch

Hi Tor Wildlife Management Area continued:

makes a great five-day backpacking trip. The main Finger Lakes Trail runs for 557 miles between the Allegheny Mountains and the Catskill Mountains. Information and maps on all segments of the Finger Lakes Trail can be purchased from the Finger Lakes Trail Conference.

Within Hi Tor property, the easiest skiing is on the old logging roads which are gated to keep cars out year-round. Parking on Bassett Road or Brink Hill Road will require a gradual uphill climb to the top of the plateau.

The parking area off East Hill Road and the blue trail heading north are on private property. George Fraley provides a paved parking area at the beginning of his driveway (6486 East Hill Road). Follow the blue blazes from the parking area around the edge of his property for the hiking trail, or follow the driveway past a large house with garages (home of OCCS - Ontario County Conservation Society) for the more graded ski trail. Gently graded switchbacks are labeled for skiing up the hill. They diverge from the blue-blazed hiking trail but follow the same general route. Both routes pass a camping area with 2 shelters and an outhouse midway up the hill.

Visit Camp 2 for a panoramic view of Canandaigua Lake in the valley far below. **Camping is not allowed** in the Hi Tor Wildlife Management Area except by organized groups during non-hunting seasons with a written permit from the DEC Regional Wildlife Manager in Avon, or on George Fraley's property with his permission.

Trail	Distance
Bassett Rd. parking to Camp 2	1.8 miles
Bassett Rd. parking to Brink Hill Rd. parking	2.5 miles
Camp 1 to Camp 2	1.1 miles
Camp 1 to 6486 East Hill Road	2.3 miles

Eskimos have at least 32 different words to describe snow:

pun	snow
pukak	sugar snow
apingaut	first snowfall
pokaktok	salt-like snow
aput	spread-out snow
miulik	sleet
kanik	frost
massak	snow mixed with water
kanigruak	frost on a living surface
auksalak	melting snow
aniuk	snow for melting into water
ayak	snow on clothes
kannik	snowflake
akillukkak	soft snow
nutagak	powder snow
milik	very soft snow
aniu	packed snow
mitailak	soft snow covering an opening in an ice floe
ananiuvak	snowbank
natigvik	snowdrift
sillik	hard, crusty snow
kimaugruk	snowdrift that blocks something
kiksrukak	glazed snow in a thaw
mauya	snow that can be broken through
perksertok	drifting snow
akelrorak	newly drifting snow
katiksunik	light snow
mavsa	snowdrift overhead and about to fall
katiksugnik	light snow deep enough for walking
kaiyuglak	rippled surface of snow
apuuak	snow patch
sisuuk	avalanche

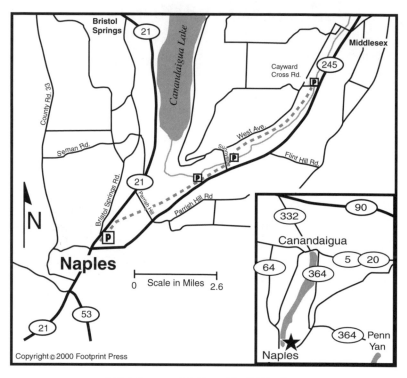

Middlesex Valley Rail Trail

41.

Middlesex Valley Rail Trail

Location:	Naples, Yates County
Directions:	Follow Route 21 along the west side of Canandaigua Lake. Just north of Naples there will be a large, dirt, pull-off area along Route 21, past the intersection of County Road 12.
Length:	6.8 miles one-way
Difficulty:	Novice
Terrain:	Gradual slope
Trail Markings:	None
Uses:	Skiing, Snowshoeing, Hiking
Amenities:	None
Admission:	Free
Dogs:	OK on leash
Hours:	Dawn to dusk
Contact:	Regional Wildlife Manager NYS Department of Environmental Conservation 6274 East Avon-Lima Road, Avon, New York 14414 (716) 226-2466 http://www.dec.state.ny.us

For Snow Conditions Call: None

The official name of this trail is the Lehigh Valley Trail. However, because other sections of the Lehigh are open for recreation, we've called it by its historical name. The trail has a slight but steady grade—uphill heading north and downhill heading south. Best of all, being in a rural area, there are only 2 road crossings in its entire length. Along the way you'll find scenery that you won't see on any other rail trail. You'll ride through Middlesex Valley with the towering hills of Naples on either side. Most of the rail bed is a raised platform through a wetland.

The Middlesex Valley Railroad first provided service between Naples and Stanley in 1892. The line was later extended to Geneva. In 1895, the rail line was purchased by the Lehigh Valley Railroad. Service continued until 1970, when the line was abandoned due to competition from trucks and cars for the freight of coal, building materials, farm equipment, apples, grapes, beans, etc. Most of the land reverted to private ownership. This portion of the rail trail is owned by New York State as part of the Hi Tor Wildlife Management Area. It is a public hunting ground, so avoid using the trail during hunting season.

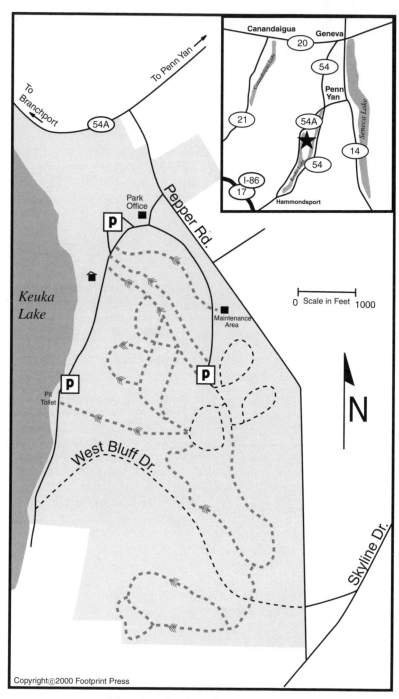

Keuka Lake State Park

42.

Keuka Lake State Park

Location:	Branchport, Yates County
Directions:	From Penn Yan at the northern end of Keuka Lake, head west on Route 54A. Turn south on Pepper Road.
Length:	7 miles of trails and unplowed roads
Difficulty:	Intermediate, Advanced
Terrain:	Hilly
Trail Markings:	None
Uses:	Skiing, Snowshoeing, Hiking
Amenities:	Restroom (pit toilet at boat launch)
Admission:	Free during winter
Dogs:	OK on leash
Hours:	Dawn to dusk
Contact:	Keuka Lake State Park 3370 Pepper Road, Bluff Point, NY 14478 (315) 536-3666

For Snow Conditions Call: (315) 536-3666

The 621 acres of Keuka Lake State Park are located in the heart of wine country. Enjoy the trails with views of vineyard-covered slopes reaching down to a frozen expanse of the crooked lake. The trails pass through woodlands and range from 714 to 1,200 feet in elevation.

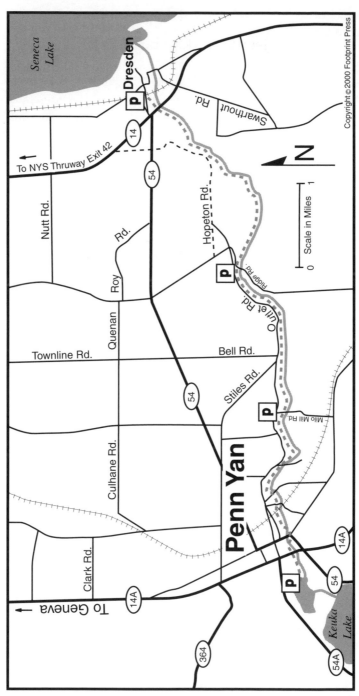

Keuka Lake Outlet Trail

43.

Keuka Lake Outlet Trail

Location:	Dresden to Penn Yan, Yates County
Directions:	From Route 14 south along the west side of Seneca Lake, turn left (E) at Route 54 heading toward Main Street, Dresden. There is a Citgo gas station and the Crossroads Ice Cream Shop at the corner. At the Crossroads Ice Cream Shop, take an immediate right onto Seneca Street. Parking is on your right just before the railroad tracks.
	Or, in Penn Yan park at Marsh Development Project – Little League Baseball on Elm Street (Route 54A).
Length:	7.5 miles one way
Difficulty:	Novice
Terrain:	Gradual slope
Trail Markings:	Green-and-white metal "Trail" signs
Uses:	Skiing, Snowshoeing, Hiking, Snowmobiling
Amenities:	Outhouses
Admission:	Free
Dogs:	OK on leash
Hours:	Dawn to dusk
Contact:	Friends of the Outlet
	PO Box 65, Dresden, NY 14441

For Snow Conditions Call: None

The strip of land you will be skiing from Seneca Lake to Keuka Lake is steeped in history. You'll see the evidence of places and events from several bygone eras as you head westward.

In the middle of the nineteenth century, two fingers of water connected the 274-foot drop between Keuka and Seneca Lakes, they were, the outlet to power mills and the Crooked Lake Canal for boat traffic. A dam and guardhouse in Penn Yan controlled the water flow to both. The outlet, which still carries water from one lake to the next, was formed by a ground fault in the Tully limestone allowing water to run between the two lakes. Along its banks are remnants of the many mills that once harnessed the waterpower.

The first white settlers arrived in this area around 1788, attracted by the reliable water source at the outlet. In 1789, Seneca Mill was built along the raging waters of Keuka Lake Outlet to grind flour with a 26-foot, overshot flywheel. From then until 1827, a small religious group called the Society of Universal Friends built 12 dams and many mills that helped make the area a thriving community. The mills and shops produced flour (gristmills), lumber (sawmills), tool handles, linseed oil, plaster, and liquor (distilleries).

Keuka Lake Outlet Trail continued:

There were two triphammer forges, eight fulling and carding mills, tanneries, and weavers making cotton and wool cloth. By 1835, 30 to 40 mills were in operation. But, by 1900, only 5 mills remained, mainly making paper from straw. The last water-turbine mill ceased operation in 1968.

In 1833, New York State opened the Crooked Lake Canal to span the 6 miles between the two lakes and move farm products to eastern markets. The canal was 4 feet deep and had 27 wooden locks. It took a vessel 6 hours to journey through the canal. As business boomed in the mills, the state widened and deepened the canal and replaced the wooden locks with stone. But, the canal lost money every year of its 44-year history, so in 1877, the state auctioned off all of the machinery and stone. Only the towpath remained.

In 1844, the Fall Brook Railroad was built on the towpath. Initially operated by the Penn Yan and New York Railway Company, it eventually became part of the New York Central System. Railway men called it the "Corkscrew Railway" because of its countless twists and turns. The line operated until 1972, when the tracks were washed out by the flood from Hurricane Agnes.

A local group interested in recreational use of the ravine convinced the town of Penn Yan to buy the property in 1981. Since then, it has been developed and maintained by a volunteer group called the Friends of the Outlet. Trail signs and outhouses were recently added along the route.

There is a slight upward grade (274 feet total) from Dresden to Penn Yan. You probably won't notice it until you turn around to glide back home—all of a sudden the going gets easier. That's why it's best to start in Dresden and do the uphill grade while you're fresh and energetic.

Reference Guides: Purchase an illustrated guide to the Keuka Lake Outlet for $1.00 from the Yates County Historian, 110 Court Street, Penn Yan, NY 14527. A packet of information on the history of the mill sites, canal, and railroad of the Keuka Lake Outlet is available for $3.00 at stores in Penn Yan.

Allegany
& Steuben
Counties

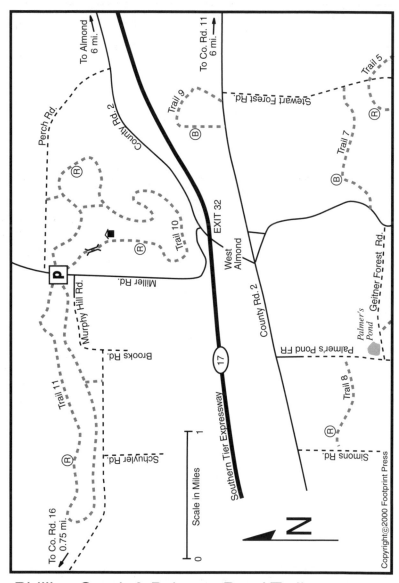

Phillips Creek & Palmers Pond Trails (North Section)

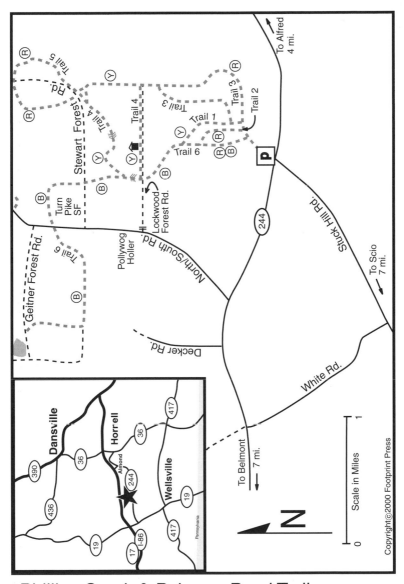

Phillips Creek & Palmers Pond Trails (South Section)

44.

Phillips Creek & Palmers Pond State Forests

Location: West Almond, Allegany County

Directions: From Route 17 (I-86) take exit 32 and follow Miller Road 2
miles north to the parking area for Trails 10 & 11. From Route
17 (I-86) take exit 32 and head south on South Road. It will
turn into North Road then meet Route 244. Turn east on 244
then left at the blue "Parking Area" sign for the lower trails.

Length: 28 miles of trails

Difficulty: Novice, Intermediate, Advanced

Terrain: Varied

Trail Markings: Number signs, 3-inch round colored markers, blazes

Uses: Skiing, Snowshoeing, Snowmobiling

Amenities: None

Admission: Free

Dogs: OK

Hours: Dawn to dusk

Contact: NYS DEC, Region 9
5425 County Route 48, Belmont, NY 14813
(716) 268-5392

For Snow Conditions Call: None

This area is a horse paradise in summer and a ski paradise in winter. The trails are
closed to horses from October 1 through May 31. The trail network is well-marked
and winds through a mixed forest.

Make a holiday of your trip by staying at Pollywog Holler, a rustic ecolodge nestled on a stream in the woods, off South Road. Even if you don't spend a night,
wander the grounds which are filled with abstract sculptures from Alfred State College Students. (1-800-291-9668, pwholler@aol.com).

Trail	Distance	Marking	Difficulty	Uses Allowed
Trail 1	1.46 miles	Yellow	Novice	Ski, Snowshoe
Trail 2	1.25 miles	Red	Novice	Ski, Snowshoe
Trail 3	2.06 miles	Red	Intermediate	Ski, Snowshoe
Trail 4	2.96 miles	Yellow	Intermediate	Ski, Snowshoe
Trail 5	1.85 miles	Red	Advanced	Ski, Snowshoe
Trail 6	4.65 miles	Blue	——	Snowshoe
Trail 7	1.5 miles	Blue	——	Snowshoe
Trail 8	0.9 mile	Red	——	Snowshoe, Snowmobile
Trail 9	1.25 miles	Blue	Novice	Ski, Snowshoe, Snowmobile
Trail 10	5.12 miles	Red	Advanced	Ski, Snowshoe, Snowmobile
Trail 11	4.96 miles	Red	Advanced	Ski, Snowshoe, Snowmobile

 # What makes snow squeak when you walk on it?

Glaciologists (people who peer through microscopes at snowflakes) tell us that at cold temperatures, such as below $20\,^0F$, soft, wet snowflakes harden into abrasive ice crystals. The squeak you hear is the collective sound of thousands of these ice crystals colliding when compressed under your foot.

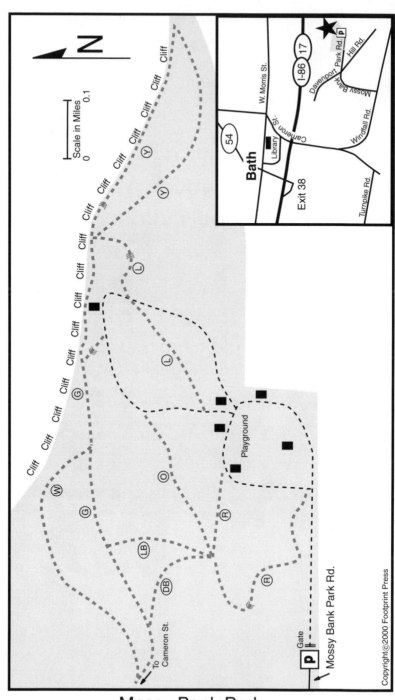

Mossy Bank Park

45.

Mossy Bank Park

Location:	Bath, Steuben County
Directions:	From Route 17 (I-86) take exit 38 to Route 54 N. Turn right onto W. Morris Street then bear right at the "Y" following a sign for bike route 17. Pass the library on the right then turn right just before Fagan's Furniture onto Cameron Street. Continue west under the railroad tracks and I-86, and over the Cohocton River. Follow the green and white signs to Mossy Bank Park and park at the end of the plowed road.
Length:	3.2 miles of trails
Difficulty:	Novice, Intermediate
Terrain:	Varied (mostly flat)
Trail Markings:	Colored blazes
Uses:	Skiing, Snowshoeing, Hiking
Amenities:	Picnic pavilions
Admission:	Free
Dogs:	OK
Hours:	10 AM to 10 PM daily
Contact:	Village of Bath, NY PO Box 668, 110 Liberty Street, Bath, NY 14810 (607) 776-3811

For Snow Conditions Call: None

Some say this park offers the "best views in western New York." It's hard to dispute this claim as you stand on the edge of a cliff overlooking Bath and the Cohocton River valley. Even without the panoramic view, this place would be special. The trails cross through hemlock forests and are easy-to-follow. Most are on the upland portion of the park and are fairly flat. Some head downhill a bit to the lowland section, perched above the cliff. These have a bit more hills. The park is officially closed in winter but skiers and snowshoers are allowed to enjoy this quiet park at their own risk.

Trail	Distance	Terrain
Unplowed Roads	0.9 mile	Flat
Red Trail	0.4 mile loop	Mild hills
Orange Trail	0.2 mile	Flat
Light Blue Trail	0.1 mile	Mild hills
Dark Blue Trail	0.1 mile	Mild hills
Green Trail	0.5 mile	Hill at north end
White Trail	0.3 mile	Mild hills
Lavender Trail	0.2 mile	Hill at north end
Yellow Trail	0.5 mile loop	Gradual hill

Roman emperors are alleged to have sent slaves to mountain tops to bring back fresh show which was then flavored and served as part of their famous food orgies.

Tioga &
Chemung
Counties

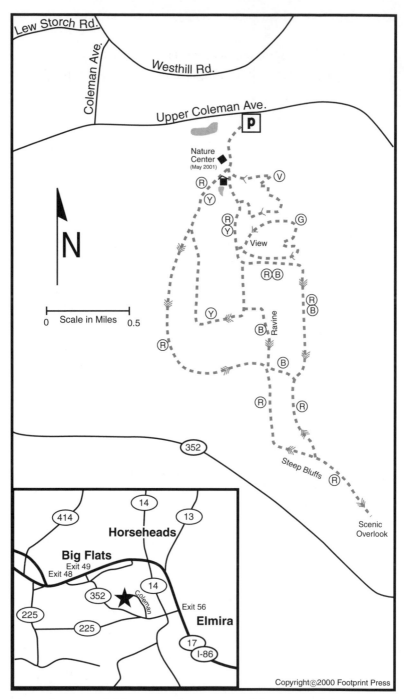

Tanglewood Nature Center - Gleason Meadows

46.

Tanglewood Nature Center
Gleason Meadows & Frenchman's Bluff

Location:	Elmira, Chemung County
Directions:	From Route 17 (I-86) take exit 48 and head east on Route 352. Turn left onto Coleman Avenue. At the "T," turn left on Upper Coleman Avenue. Gleason Meadows will be on the right.
Length:	7 miles of trails
Difficulty:	Intermediate, Advanced
Terrain:	Steep hills
Trail Markings:	White sign "Tanglewood Nature Center - Gleason Meadows" at parking lot Colored blazes on trails
Uses:	Skiing, Snowshoeing, Hiking
Amenities:	None (A nature center with warming hut & restrooms is planned for spring 2001 completion.)
Admission:	Free
Dogs:	Pets NOT allowed
Hours:	Dawn to dusk
Contact:	Tanglewood Nature Center Museum PO Box 117, Elmira, NY 14902 (607) 732-6060

For Snow Conditions Call: (607) 732-6060

Gleason Meadows covers 172 acres of meadow, scrubland, and woods. The high elevation means this area is likely to have snow when other areas are bare. Pick a loop to fit your time and ability. The 3-mile Red Oak Trail leads to a scenic view of the Chemung River valley originally produced during the Ice Age and now enhanced by the river.

The Frenchman who's bluff you'll enjoy was Eugene Berthod. He was a central figure in the early settlement of Big Flats. He grew vegetable crops for sale, ran a hotel for weary travelers, and even provided French language lessons for local children.

Trail Name	Blazes	Distance	Level of Difficulty
Red Oak Trail	Red	3.1 miles	Advanced
Yellow Warbler Trail	Yellow	2.0 miles	Advanced
Blue Bird Trail	Blue	2.0 miles	Advanced
President's Trail	Green	1.4 miles	Intermediate
Whitetail Trail	Violet	1.0 mile	Intermediate

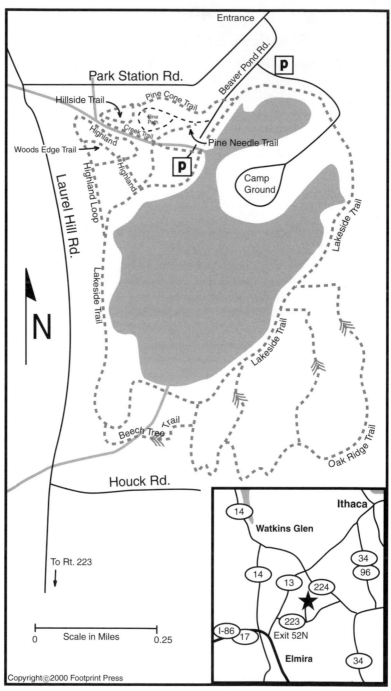

Park Station Recreation Area

47.

Park Station Recreation Area

Location:	Erin, Chemung County
Directions:	From Route 224 in the northeast corner of Chemung County, turn west on Route 223, then right (N) on Austin Hill Road. Turn right (W) on Park Station Road and follow it to the recreation area.
Length:	6.2 miles of trails
Difficulty:	Novice, Intermediate, Advanced
Terrain:	Flat areas & hilly areas
Trail Markings:	Yellow on black skier signs, arrow signs
Uses:	Skiing, Snowshoeing, Hiking
Amenities:	Porta-potties near parking, restroom in camping area
	Year round camping
Admission:	Free ($6/vehicle Memorial Day to Labor Day)
Dogs:	Pets NOT allowed
Hours:	9 AM to dusk
Contact:	Chemung County Parks, Recreation and Youth Bureau
	2 West Beaver Pond Road, Erin, NY 14838
	(607) 739-9164

For Snow Conditions Call: (607) 739-9164

Park Station Recreation Area sits on top of high hills. The land surrounds a large pond (formed by damming a stream) which is popular with ice fishermen and ice skaters. It forms a pleasant backdrop for skiers and snowshoers.

In the late 1800s Park Hill was named to honor residents Robert & Alexander Park. After a railway line was built in 1892 the community boomed and became known as Park Station. Park Station's population dwindled with the passing of the railroad and timber industry. In 1979 the creek was dammed as part of a plan to improve area soil and water resources and the area became a public recreation center.

Trail	Distance	Level of Difficulty
Lakeside Trail	2.7 miles	Novice
Pine Cone Trail	0.4 mile	Intermediate
Creek Trail	0.3 mile	Intermediate
Hillside Trail	0.1 mile	Intermediate
Pine Path	<0.1 mile	Intermediate
Pine Needle Trail	0.1 mile	Novice
Highland Loop	0.7 mile	Advanced
Woods Edge Trail	0.1 mile	Intermediate
Highland Trail	0.1 mile	Intermediate
Beech Tree Trail	0.3 mile	Intermediate
Oak Ridge Trail	1.3 miles	Advanced

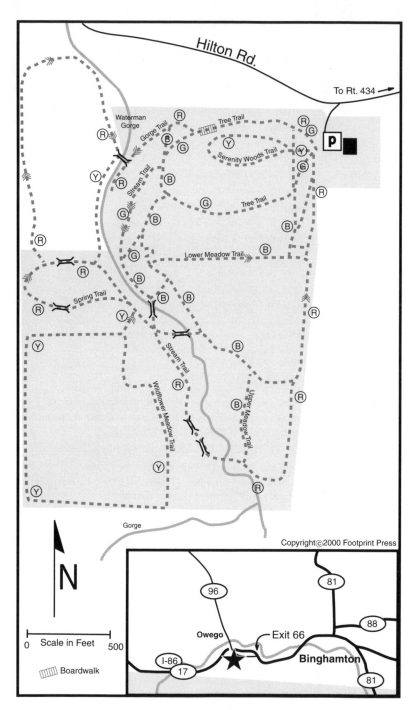

Waterman Conservation Education Center

48.

Waterman Conservation Education Center

Location:	Apalachin, Tioga County
Directions:	From Route 17 (I-86), take exit 66 (Apalachin). Go west on Route 434 for 1.5 miles. Turn left on Hilton Road. The center will be on the left.
Length:	5 miles of trails
Difficulty:	Novice, Intermediate
Terrain:	Gentle hills
Trail Markings:	2-inch round, plastic, colored markers
Uses:	Skiing, Snowshoeing, Hiking
Amenities:	Warming hut & restrooms (interpretive building) Ski ($14/day) and snowshoe ($5/day) rentals
Admission:	Free
Dogs:	Pets NOT allowed
Hours:	Dawn to dusk
Contact:	Waterman Conservation Education Center 403 Hilton Road, PO Box 377, Apalachin, NY 13732 (607) 625-4073 www.tier.net/waterman

For Snow Conditions Call: (607) 625-4073

The Waterman Conservation Eduction Center exists due to the desire of community citizens to preserve wildlife habitat. Lolita Waterman donated a portion of her family farm as a memorial for her late husband, Fred L. Waterman and volunteers worked to establish the interpretive center and grounds.

The interpretative building now houses a museum where visitors will find numerous exhibits and displays about local wildlife. The museum building also houses the Center's Nature Shop, classroom space, a reference library and offices. Waterman Center holds classes year-round on a variety of nature, conservation, and outdoor recreation topics.

The trails run through young woods and meadows on a hilltop and cross a stream gully. The trails east of the stream are wide and easy to follow. West of the stream they're a bit more of a challenge.

Trail	Marker	Distance	Level of Difficulty
Serenity Woods Trail	Yellow	0.2 mile	Novice
Tree Trail	Green	0.5 mile	Novice
Gorge Trail	Red	0.1 mile	Intermediate
Spring Trail	Red	0.3 mile	Novice
Wildflower Meadow	Yellow	1.5 miles	Novice
Stream Trail	Green/Red	0.5 mile	Novice
Upper Meadow Trail	Red/Blue	0.3 mile	Novice
Lower Meadow Trail	Blue	0.5 mile	Novice

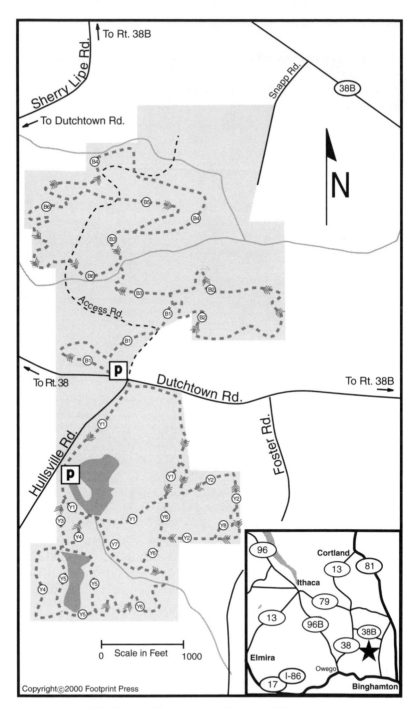

Oakley Corners State Forest

49.

Oakley Corners State Forest

Location:	Newark Valley & Owego, Tioga County
Directions:	From Route 38, turn east onto Wade Hollow Road. Continue straight as it turns into Dutchtown Road.
Length:	16 miles of trails
Difficulty:	Novice, Intermediate, Advanced
Terrain:	Modest hills (1,150-1,550 feet elevation)
Trail Markings:	Colored & numbered circular trail markers
Uses:	Skiing, Snowshoeing, Hiking
Amenities:	None
Admission:	Free
Dogs:	OK on leash
Hours:	Dawn to dusk
Contact:	NYS Department of Environmental Conservation 1285 Fisher Ave., Cortland, NY 13045-1090 (607) 753-3095 ext. 221

For Snow Conditions Call: None

Once farmland and pasture, this 1,042-acre forest was planted with pine, spruce, cedar, and larch in 1936. It is now managed for forest product harvesting and recreation.

The yellow trails sit at higher elevation, most above 1,400 feet, and usually have the best snow cover. Most trails are narrow woods trails. Trails Y1, Y2, Y3, and Y4 utilize old logging roads.

Trail	Distance	Level of Difficulty
Yellow 1	1.9 miles	Novice
Yellow 2	1.0 mile	Intermediate
Yellow 3	0.3 mile	Novice
Yellow 4	0.8 mile	Novice
Yellow 5	0.9 mile	Novice
Yellow 6	1.1 miles	Advanced
Yellow 7	0.7 mile	Intermediate
Yellow 8	0.1 mile	Intermediate
Blue 1	1.0 mile	Intermediate
Blue 2	1.8 miles	Advanced
Blue 3	0.7 mile	Advanced
Blue 4	1.6 miles	Advanced
Blue 5	1.0 mile	Intermediate
Blue 6	1.0 mile	Advanced
Access Road	1.8 miles	Intermediate

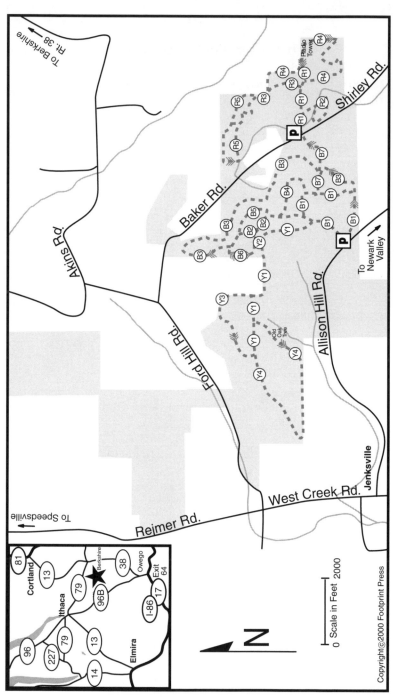

Jenksville State Forest

50.

Jenksville State Forest

Location:	Berkshire & Newark Valley, Tioga County
Directions:	From Route 38, north of Newark Valley, turn left (E) on Tappan Road. Turn right on Howard Hill Road then bear right on Shirley Road.
Length:	12 miles of trails
Difficulty:	Novice, Intermediate, Advanced
Terrain:	Modest hills, 1,300-1,650 feet elevation
Trail Markings:	Colored & numbered circular trail markers
Uses:	Skiing, Snowshoeing, Hiking
Amenities:	None
Admission:	Free
Dogs:	OK on leash
Hours:	Dawn to dusk
Contact:	NYS Department of Environmental Conservation 1285 Fisher Ave., Cortland, NY 13045-1090 (607) 753-3095 ext. 221

For Snow Conditions Call: None

Once farmland and pasture, this 1,349-acre forest was planted with pine, spruce, fir, cedar, oak and larch in 1940. It is now managed for forest product harvesting and recreation.

The blue trails sit at 1,690 feet elevation and usually have the best snow cover. Most trails are narrow woods trails. Trails R1, B1, B7, and most yellow trails utilize old logging roads. An open-grown, red oak tree along Y4 is 60 inches in diameter and approximately 200 years old. The westernmost tip of Y4 affords a scenic view of Jenksville and the valley to the south.

Trail	Marking	Distance	Level of Difficulty
Red 1	R1	0.5 mile	Novice
Red 2	R2	0.5 mile	Novice
Red 3	R3	0.1 mile	Novice
Red 4	R4	1.4 mile	Novice
Red 5	R5	1.1 miles	Intermediate
Blue 1	B1	1.1 miles	Intermediate
Blue 2	B2	0.4 mile	Novice
Blue 3	B3	2.1 miles	Advanced
Blue 4	B4	0.4 miles	Intermediate
Blue 5	B5	0.3 mile	Intermediate
Blue 6	B6	0.4 mile	Advanced
Blue 7	B7	0.4 mile	Intermediate
Yellow 1	Y1	1.3 miles	Intermediate
Yellow 2	Y2	0.1 mile	Intermediate
Yellow 3	Y3	0.7 mile	Intermediate

Snowshoeing is fun for the whole family —
at least Michael and Carol Weber
and their kids Alec, Andrew, and M.J. think so.

Schuyler &
Tompkins
Counties

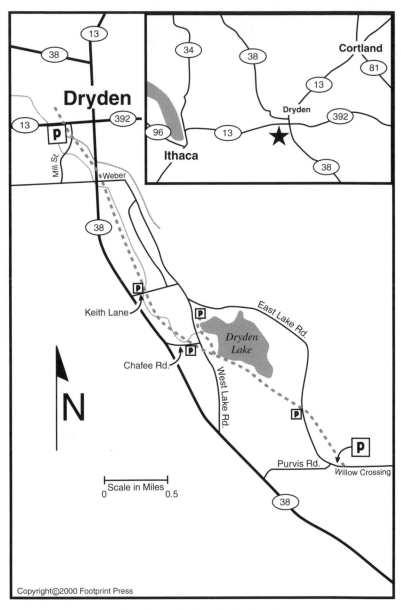

Dryden Lake Park Trail

51.
Dryden Lake Park Trail

Location:	Dryden, Tompkins & Cortland Counties
Directions:	From Ithaca, follow Route 13 east to Dryden. Park at or near the Dryden Agway with permission (59 West Main Street, across from Rochester Street).
Length:	8.2 miles (one way)
Difficulty:	Novice
Terrain:	Flat
Trail Markings:	Square blue-and-white metal signs "Dryden Lake Park Trail," and mile markers every half mile along the trail
Uses:	Skiing, Snowshoeing, Hiking
Amenities:	None
Admission:	Free
Dogs:	OK on leash
Hours:	Dawn to dusk
Contact:	Town of Dryden 65 East Main Street, Dryden, NY 13053 (607) 844-8619 www.dryden.ny.us

For Snow Conditions Call: None

The Southern Central Railroad was built in 1865 to connect Sayre, Pennsylvania to Auburn. It became part of the Lehigh Valley System and was abandoned in 1976. The tracks were taken up and sold for scrap in 1979.

Dryden Lake Park is 0.1 mile north of the West Lake Road crossing. This park offers ice fishing access, a pavilion, and an observation deck over the lake. The area was once an Indian campground and home of an early sawmill and railroad ice station.

Interpretive signs along this easy-to-follow trail offer information on the animals and plants that inhabit the area. Birds are abundant, and beaver activity is evident if you watch carefully.

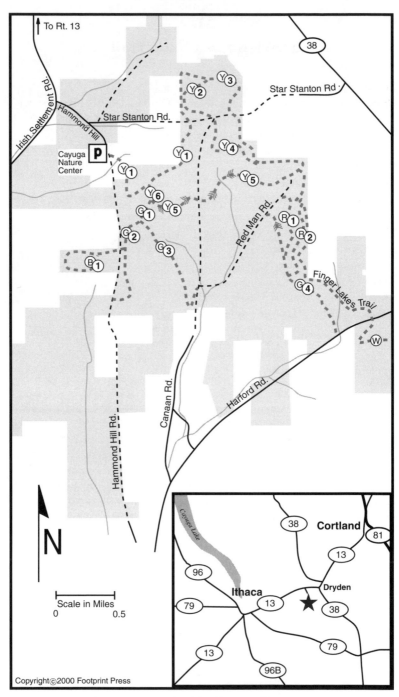

Hammond Hill State Forest

52.

Hammond Hill State Forest

Location:	Dryden, Tompkins County
Directions:	From Ithaca, head east on Route 13. Pass Yellow Barn Hill Road and turn south on Irish Settlement Road. Turn left (E) on Hammond Hill Road. Follow it to the end.
Length:	11 miles of trails
Difficulty:	Novice, Intermediate, Advanced
Terrain:	Hilly
Trail Markings:	Numbered trail junctions, round plastic markers (colored and numbered)
Uses:	Skiing, Snowshoeing, Hiking, Snowmobiling
Amenities:	None
	Camping is allowed 150 feet from water, roads, or trails
Admission:	Free
Dogs:	OK
Hours:	Dawn to dusk
Contact:	NYS Department of Environmental Conservation
	1285 Fisher Avenue, Cortland, NY 13045
	(607) 753-3095 ext. 215
	www.dec.state.ny.us

For Snow Conditions Call: None

Hammond Hill was established as a state forest between 1935 and 1950 in an effort to reduce soil erosion, produce forest products, and provide recreational opportunities. Once depleted farmland, it was planted with thousands of pine, spruce, larch, maple, ash, cherry, and oak seedlings. Today it it heavily forested.

Sitting above 1,800 feet in elevation, the network of trails are well suited for winter fun. And, it's a busy place all winter long—heavily used by Cayuga Nordic Ski Club, Cornell Nordic Ski Team, and many others. A snowmobile trail (marked green) and the Finger Lakes hiking trail (white blazed) cross the forest.

Yellow Trails - 5.6 miles on old logging roads and fire lanes

Trail	Level of Difficulty	Distance
Y1	Intermediate	1.9 miles
Y2	Novice	0.6 mile
Y3	Intermediate	0.6 mile (scenic view of Dryden Lake)
Y4	Intermediate	1.0 mile
Y5	Advanced	1.3 miles
Y6	Novice	0.2 mile

Blue Trail - 1 mile

Trail	Level of Difficulty	Distance
B1	Novice	1 mile

Hammond Hill State Forest continued:

Red Trails - 1.7 miles used by Cornell Nordic Ski team. Cut wide for skating.

Trail	Level of Difficulty	Distance
R1	Advanced	0.6 mile
R2	Advanced	1.1 miles

Green Snowmobile Trails - 5.6 miles, can be used by skiers

Trail	Level of Difficulty	Distance
G1	Novice	0.2 mile
G2	Novice	0.8 mile
G3	Intermediate	0.9 mile
G4	Intermediate	1.2 miles

Finger Lakes Trail (white blazes) 3.2 miles

Forest Access and Seasonal Use Roads, 6.2 miles, snowmobiling is primary use but skiing is allowed.

Is colorful snow safe to eat?

Red, white, and blue snow may be edible but avoid the yellow stuff. The slight red color in some snow comes from harmless algae. White and blue are normal snow colors. White snow can appear blue when you look up at it from below, like from the inside of an igloo or ice cave. It's common knowledge what makes snow yellow and if you find snow in any other colors it's probably contaminated and best avoided.

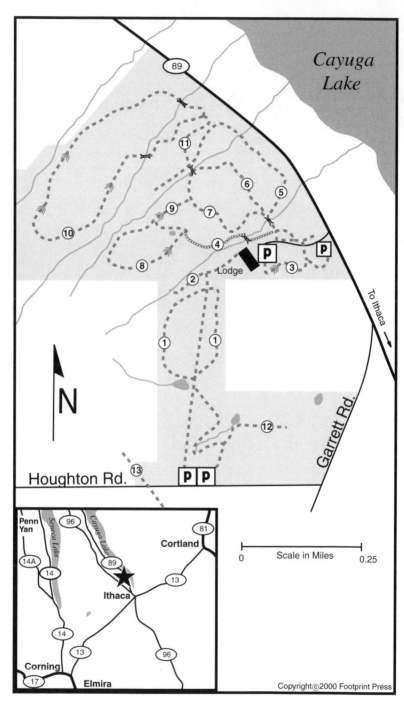

Cayuga Nature Center

53.
Cayuga Nature Center

Location:	Ithaca, Tompkins County
Directions:	From Ithaca, head north for 6 miles on Route 89, along the west side of Cayuga Lake. Cayuga Nature Center will be on the left.
Length:	5 miles of trails
Difficulty:	Novice, Intermediate
Terrain:	Hilly
Trail Markings:	Colored plastic markers
Uses:	Skiing, Snowshoeing, Hiking
Amenities:	Warming hut (visitor center open Monday - Friday, 8 AM - 5 PM)
	Restrooms (in visitor center & privy on Trail 11)
Admission:	Free
Dogs:	NOT allowed
Hours:	Dawn to dusk
Contact:	Cayuga Nature Center
	1420 Taughannock Blvd., Ithaca, NY 14850
	(607) 273-6260
	www.fcoinet.com/cnc

For Snow Conditions Call: (607) 273-6260

Cayuga Nature Center is an environmental education center situated on 135 acres of woods, open fields, gorges, and waterfalls. An adjoining farm has a land-lab, agriculture and forestry exhibits, and live farm animals. The farm fences are electrified so, keep your distance. Public nature programs are offered every Sunday afternoon.

Trail	Distance	Level of Difficulty
1. Field Trail	0.5 mile	Novice
2. Falls Overlook Trail	0.2 mile	Novice
3. Sugarbush Trail	0.2 mile	Intermediate
4. Stream Trail	0.3 mile	Hike/snowshoe only
5. Wishing Tree Trail	0.5 mile	Novice
6. Team Challenge Trail	0.3 mile	Intermediate
7. Gorge Trail	0.3 mile	Intermediate
8. Plant Succession Trail	0.4 mile	Intermediate
9. Pond Trail	0.1 mile	Intermediate
10. Wilderness Trail	1.1 miles	intermediate
11. Privy Trail	0.2 mile	Intermediate
12. Farm Trail	0.4 mile	Novice
13. Future Black Diamond multi-use trail		

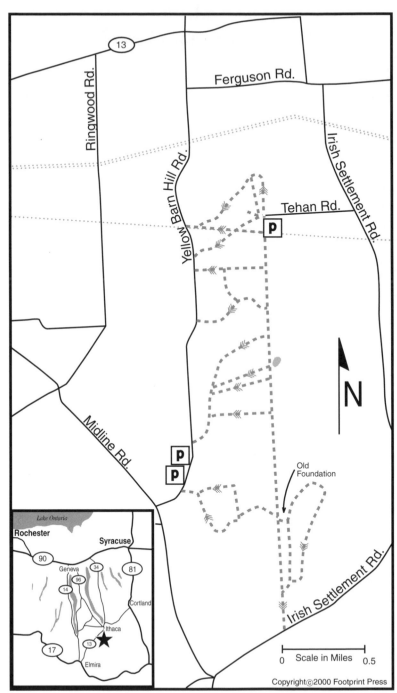

Yellow Barn State Forest

54.

Yellow Barn State Forest

Location:	Dryden, Tompkins County
Directions:	From Ithaca, head east on Route 13. Pass Yellow Barn Hill Road and turn south on Irish Settlement Road. Turn right (W) on Tehan Road. Follow it around a sharp bend, to the end.
Length:	8 miles of trails
Difficulty:	Advanced
Terrain:	Hilly
Trail Markings:	None
Uses:	Skiing, Snowshoeing, Hiking
Amenities:	None
Admission:	Free
Dogs:	OK
Hours:	Dawn to dusk
Contact:	NYS Department of Environmental Conservation
	1285 Fisher Avenue, Cortland, NY 13045
	(607) 753-3095 ext. 215
	www.dec.state.ny.us

For Snow Conditions Call: None

You'll find a challenge on these 8-foot-wide trails through the forest. That's because they traverse steep hills. The trails aren't generally good for skating and can be wet except under deep snow or after prolonged periods of cold. But, if you prefer uncrowded, challenging woods trails, this is the place to ski.

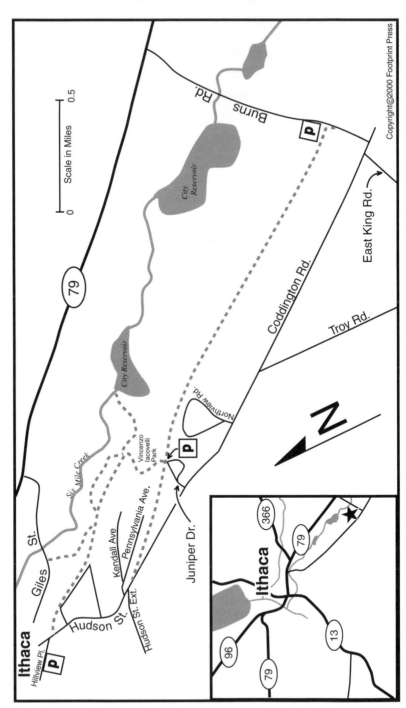

South Hill Recreation Way

160

55.
South Hill Recreation Way

Location:	Ithaca, Tompkins County
Directions:	From Ithaca, follow Route 79 east. Turn right (S) on Burns Road. Parking is on the west side of Burns Road at a sign for "South Hill Recreation Way Parking." Watch for the green-and-white, square bicycle signs.
Length:	3.3 miles of trail
Difficulty:	Novice
Terrain:	Gradual Hills
Trail Markings:	Yellow-and-brown wooden signs "South Hill Recreation Way" and mile marker signs every half mile
Uses:	Skiing, Snowshoeing, Hiking
Amenities:	Benches
Admission:	Free
Dogs:	OK on leash
Hours:	Dawn to dusk
Contact:	Town of Ithaca Highway Department 106 Seven Mile Drive, Ithaca, NY 14850 (607) 273-8035

For Snow Conditions Call: None

This trail was developed in 1993 as a NYS Environmental Quality Bond Act Project. Today, it's a gem for all of us to enjoy. It follows the abandoned rail bed of the Cayuga and Susquehanna, which was built in 1849 to haul coal from the Pennsylvania mines to a canal in Ithaca. Eventually it merged with the Delaware, Lackawanna, and Western Railroad and was abandoned in 1957.

The terrain is gradual hills, mostly downhill on the outbound leg (heading NW) and uphill for the return. You're in the Six Mile Creek Gorge. This creek is currently dammed for use as a water supply for Ithaca. Smaller paths lead off the main trail into the gorge. Numbered posts are positioned along part of the route at the western end. Along with an instructive brochure, they describe the plant communities that are hidden under a blanket of snow.

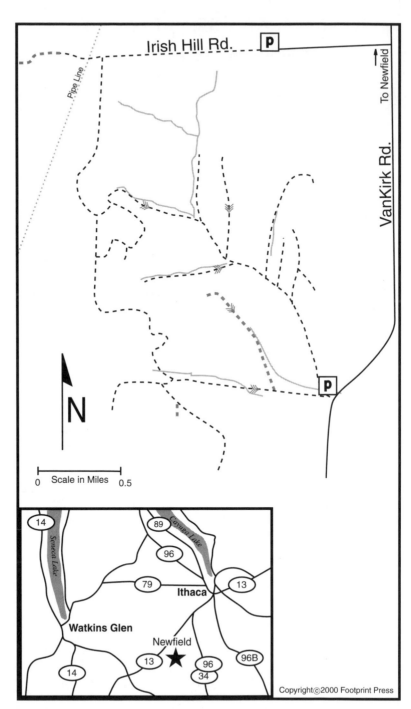

Arnot Forest

56.

Arnot Forest

Location:	Newfield, Tompkins County
Directions:	From Ithaca, take Route 13 west and exit at Newfield. Turn right on Main Street, then south on VanKirk Road at the sign for "Arnot Forest." Turn right onto Irish Hill Road and follow it to the end. Or, for the southern parking area, continue south on Van Kirk Road to the brown, wooden sign "Cornell University - Arnot Teaching & Research Forest."
Length:	12 miles of trails
Difficulty:	Intermediate, Advanced
Terrain:	Hilly
Trail Markings:	None
Uses:	Skiing, Snowshoeing, Hiking
Amenities:	None
Admission:	Free
Dogs:	OK on leash
Hours:	Dawn to dusk
Contact:	Forest Manager, Department of Natural Resources Cornell University 611 County Route 13, VanEtten, NY 14889 (607) 589-6095

For Snow Conditions Call: None

The adventure begins in the village of Newfield where you'll pass the only remaining covered bridge still in daily use in New York State. Then on to the 4,000-acre Arnot Teaching and Research Forest. It is owned by Cornell University and is used for student fieldwork, research, and extension activities. The forest is home to many ongoing demonstration projects and an active springtime maple sugaring operation.

You'll find a combination of unplowed dirt roads and trails, all winding through the woods. Once abandoned farmland and wood lots, Cornell University has owned this land since the 1920s. The public is welcome to explore the trails but please stay out of posted or restricted areas.

The covered bridge in Newfield.

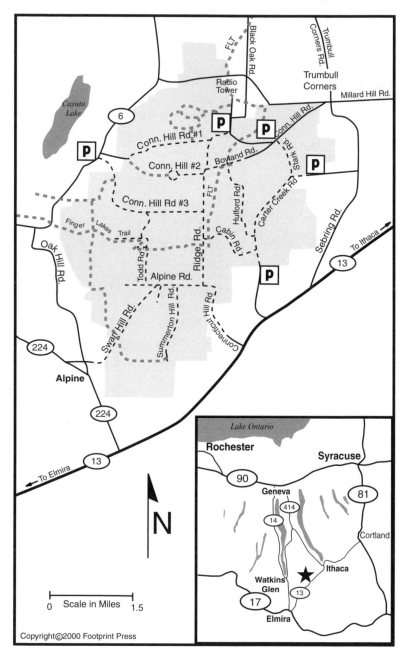

Connecticut Hill

57.
Connecticut Hill

Location:	Midway between the south ends of Seneca Lake and Cayuga Lake, 13 miles southwest of Ithaca, Schuyler and Tompkins Counties
Directions:	From Ithaca, head south on Route 13. Turn west on Millard Hill Road, 1 mile beyond the junction with Routes 34 & 96. Pass through Trumbull Corners, then turn left on Connecticut Hill Road. Park at any of the locations on the map where plowing ends.
Length:	More than 20 miles of unplowed roads and trails
Difficulty:	Advanced
Terrain:	Steep Hills
Trail Markings:	None
Uses:	Skiing, Snowshoeing, Hiking, Snowmobiling
Amenities:	None
Admission:	Free
Dogs:	OK
Hours:	Dawn to dusk
Contact:	NYS Department of Environmental Conservation 1285 Fisher Avenue, Cortland, NY 13045 (607) 753-3095 www.dec.state.ny.us

For Snow Conditions Call: None

Connecticut Hill is the largest wildlife management area in New York State, covering 11,654 acres. It is part of the Appalachian Highlands, which is distinctive as a belt of high, rough land. It often has snow when the lowlands don't. The terrain is always hilly (too many to label on the map), sometimes with steep sections as it winds on and off the plateau. Expect an aerobic workout.

Besides the steep hills, the other challenge of this area is that most roads are not labeled. You need to be able to follow the map to traverse this area successfully. Then too, you'll find that many of the roads are called Connecticut Hill Road, sometimes with a number and sometimes without.

Connecticut Hill is very popular with snowmobilers. They make wide, packed trails that are good for skating.

Indians were the first inhabitants to roam this area. They were driven out by George Washington's troops in the late 1700s. From 1800 until 1850, the land was owned by the state of Connecticut and then sold to private landowners. However, the name, Connecticut Hill, stuck.

Connecticut Hill continued:

By the mid-19th century, much of the land in this area had been cleared for cultivation and pasture. But the farms languished due to poor soil conditions, and many farms were abandoned. By 1926, only 20 of the original 109 farms remained in operation. Through the Federal Resettlement Administration, the government began buying farmland and the game refuge came into existence.

Unplowed Road/Trail	Distance	Level of Difficulty
Connecticut Hill Road #1	2.0 miles	Intermediate
Connecticut Hill Road #3	2.9 miles	Intermediate
Ridge Road	3.0 miles	Novice
Stark Road	0.7 miles	Advanced
Carter Creek Road	2.2 miles	Advanced
Todd Road	1.5 miles	Advanced
Swan Hill Road	2.0 miles	Advanced
Summerton Hill Road	1.5 miles	Advanced
Hulford Road	1.9 miles	Advanced
Finger Lakes Trail	9 miles (in Conn. Hill)	Novice to Advanced

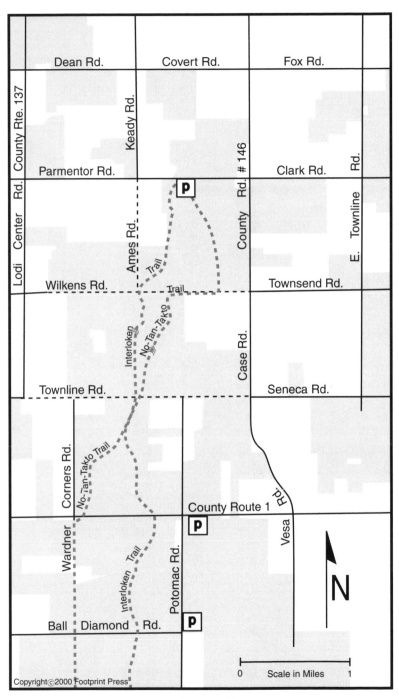

Dean Rd. Covert Rd. Fox Rd.

County Rte. 137

Keady Rd.

Parmentor Rd.

County Rd. # 146

Clark Rd.

Lodi Center Rd.

Ames Rd.

Trail

P

Wilkens Rd. Trail Townsend Rd.

E. Townline Rd.

Interloken

No-Tan-Takto

Case Rd.

Townline Rd. Seneca Rd.

Corners Rd.

No-Tan-Takto Trail

County Route 1

Vesa Rd.

P

Wardner

Interloken Trail

Potomac Rd.

P

Ball Diamond Rd.

N

0 Scale in Miles 1

Finger Lakes National Forest (North Section)

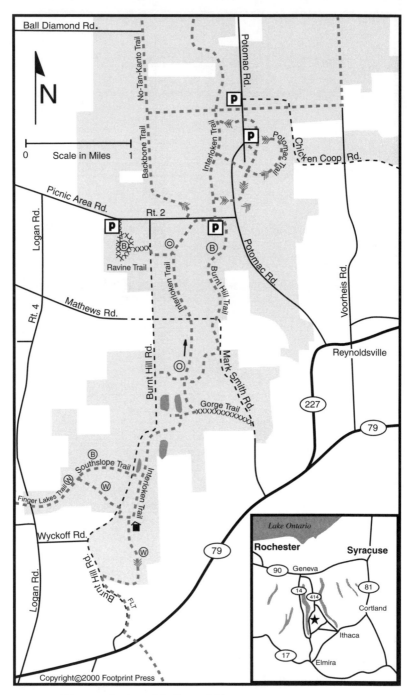

Finger Lakes National Forest (South Section)

58.

Finger Lakes National Forest

Location:	Southeast side of Seneca Lake, Schuyler & Seneca Counties
Directions:	From Route 414, head east on County Route 2 (Picnic Area Road). Pass Logan Road and Burnt Hill Road. The Blueberry Patch Campsite parking area will be on the right.
Length:	30.5 miles of skiable trails
	2 miles of snowshoe only trails
	11.7 miles of unplowed roads
Difficulty:	Novice, Intermediate
Terrain:	Varies from flat to hilly
Trail Markings:	Excellent signs at junctions, blazes along trails
Uses:	Skiing, Snowshoeing, Hiking
Amenities:	None
Admission:	Free
Dogs:	OK on leash
Hours:	Dawn to dusk
Contacts:	Finger Lakes National Forest
	5218 State Route 414, Hector, NY 14841
	(607) 546-4470
	www.fs.fed.us/r9/gmfl
	Finger Lakes Trail Conference
	P.O. Box 18048, Rochester, NY 14618-0048
	(716) 288-7191
	www.fingerlakes.net/trailsystem

For Snow Conditions Call: None

The Finger Lakes National Forest encompasses 16,036 acres of land and has over 30 miles of interconnecting trails and another 11 miles of unplowed roads that stretch through forests and fields. It also offers overnight camping and a privately owned bed-and-breakfast (Red House Country Inn B&B, Picnic Area Road, 607-546-8566) nearby, making it a perfect weekend getaway. Contact the Finger Lakes National Forest for additional information on camping.

The Iroquois Indians originally inhabited the area around the Finger Lakes National Forest. In 1790 the area was divided into 600-acre military lots and distributed among Revolutionary War veterans as payment for their services. These early settlers cleared the land for production of hay and small grains such as buckwheat. As New York City grew, a strong market for these products developed, encouraging more intensive agriculture. The farmers prospered until the middle of the nineteenth century, when a series of events occurred. These included the popularity of motorized transportation in urban centers (reducing the number of horses to be fed), gradual depletion of the soil resource, and competition from midwestern agriculture due to the opening of the Erie Canal.

Finger Lakes National Forest continued:

Between 1890 and the Great Depression, over a million acres of farmland were abandoned in south central New York State. In the 1930s it was obvious that farmers in many parts of the country could no longer make a living from their exhausted land. Environmental damage worsened as they cultivated the land more and more intensively to make ends meet. Several pieces of legislation were passed, including the Emergency Relief Act of 1933 and the Bankhead-Jones Farm Tenant Act of 1937, to address these problems. A new government agency, the Resettlement Administration, was formed to carry out the new laws. This agency not only directed the relocation of farmers to better land or other jobs, but also coordinated the purchase of marginal farmland by the federal government.

Between 1938 and 1941, over 100 farms were purchased in the Finger Lakes National Forest area and administered by the Soil Conservation Service. Because this was done on a willing-seller, willing-buyer basis, the resulting federal ownership resembled a patchwork quilt. The land was named the Hector Land Use Area and was planted with conifers and turned into grazing fields to stabilize the soil. Individual livestock owners were allowed to graze animals on the pasture land to show how less intensive agriculture could still make productive use of the land.

By the 1950s many of the objectives of the Hector Land Use Area had been met, and the public was becoming interested in the concept of multiple uses of public land. In 1954 administration responsibilities were transferred to the U.S. Forest Service. The name was changed to the Hector Ranger District, Finger Lakes National Forest, in 1985.

Today this National Forest is used for recreation, hunting, forestry, grazing of private livestock, preservation of wildlife habitat, and education and research. It is a treasure available for all to enjoy.

Trail	Markings	Distance	Level of Difficulty
Backbone Trail	Blue	5.5 miles	Novice/snowmobiles
Interloken Trail	Orange	12.0 miles	Novice
No-Tan-Takto Trail	Green	4.5 miles	Novice/snowmobiles
Burnt Hill Trail	Blue	2.5 miles	Novice/snowmobiles
Gorge Trail	Blue	1.25 miles	Hike & snowshoe only
Ravine Trail	Blue	0.75 mile	Hike & snowshoe only
Southslope Trail	Blue	4.0 miles	Novice
Finger Lakes Trail	White	2.0 miles +	Intermediate
(this is a portion of a 560-mile long trail)			

Unplowed Road	Markings	Distance	Level of Difficulty
Burnt Hill Road	Road signs	4.5 miles	Intermediate
Matthews Road	Road signs	1.2 miles	Novice
Mark Smith Road	Road signs	1.5 miles	Intermediate
Ames Road	Road signs	1.0 mile	Novice
Wilkins Road	Road signs	1.0 mile	Intermediate
Townsend Road	Road signs	1.0 mile	Novice
Seneca Road	Road signs	1.5 miles	Novice

Seneca, Cayuga, & Wayne Counties

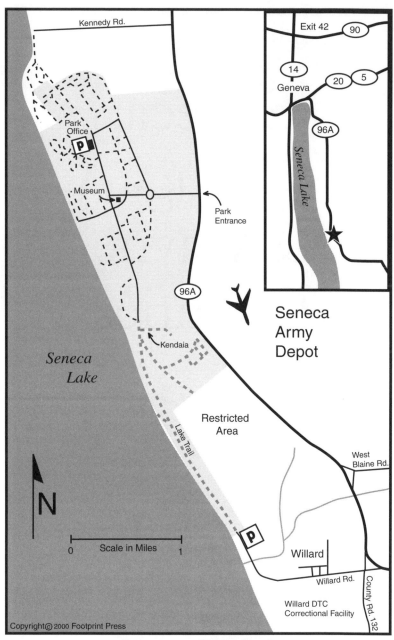

Sampson State Park

59.

Sampson State Park

Location:	East side of Seneca Lake, Seneca County
Directions:	Take Route 96A south from Geneva. Pass Sampson State Park. Where Route 96A bends east, bear right on County Road 132. Turn west on Willard Road. Follow Willard Road as it bends right and parallels the shore of Seneca Lake. The parking area is on the right of Willard Road at the barrier.
Length:	2 miles of trails
	11 miles of unplowed roads
Difficulty:	Novice, Intermediate
Terrain:	Gentle hills
Trail Markings:	None
Uses:	Skiing, Snowshoeing, Hiking
Amenities:	None
Admission:	Free (from Willard entrance year-round, at the park entrance $5 per vehicle is charged Memorial Day to Labor Day)
Dogs:	OK on leash
Hours:	Dawn to dusk
Contact:	Sampson State Park
	6096 Route 96A, Romulus, NY 14541
	(315) 585-6392

For Snow Conditions Call: None

Once a naval training station, this park was named for a Palmyra resident, Rear Admiral William T. Sampson. From the Willard parking area the trail follows the lakeshore on an abandoned road bed, gradually climbing north for 1.6 miles to Kendaia (once an agricultural settlement of the Seneca Indians). Loop around on the trail south of Kendaia, or continue north from the Lake Trail and explore the unplowed roads of Sampson State Park.

For the Novice section, park behind the park office and explore the unplowed road network at the north end of the park. In the summer this is a busy place with an active campground and marina. But, in winter, you're likely to have the place to yourself.

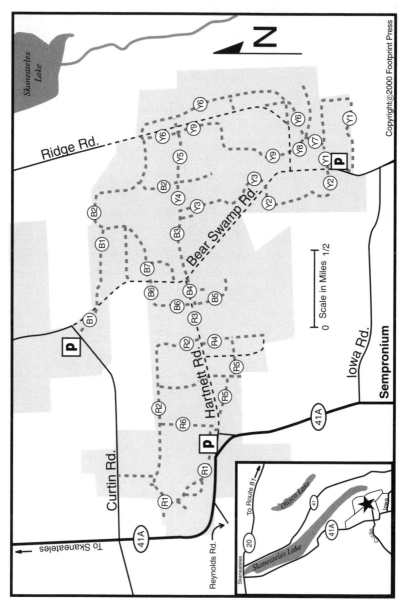

Bear Swamp State Forest

60.

Bear Swamp State Forest

Location:	Southwest end of Skaneateles Lake, Cayuga County
Directions:	From Skaneateles, head south on Route 41A. Pass Curtin Road and Reynolds Road. Turn left on the next unmarked dirt road. A brown and yellow DEC sign is on the right side of Route 41A, "Bear Swamp State Forest." Park at the end of the plowed area.
Length:	13 miles of trails
Difficulty:	Intermediate
Terrain:	Hilly
Trail Markings:	Round red, blue, and yellow trail markers
Uses:	Skiing, Snowshoeing, Hiking
Amenities:	None
Admission:	Free
Dogs:	OK
Hours:	Dawn to dusk
Contact:	NYS Department of Environmental Conservation 1285 Fisher Avenue, Cortland, NY 13045 (607) 753-3095 http://www.dec.state.ny.us

For Snow Conditions Call: None

Over 10,000 years ago the glaciers sculpted the Finger Lakes, leaving steep valley walls and flat-topped ridges. Native Americans used this area as hunting grounds. After the Revolutionary War, veterans and their families cleared the forests and settled the area. Farming continued through the Civil War and slowly declined as the soil was depleted, until the Great Depression of 1929 hastened farm abandonment. As with other State Forest land, this land was purchased in the 1930s and replanted by the Civilian Conservation Corps with red pine, Norway spruce, and larch. You'll pass through these replanted forests, now a mix of conifers and hardwoods.

Bear Swamp State Forest is managed to maintain wildlife habitat, harvest wood products, and encourage recreational uses. The trails are well marked with round trail markers. Please stay on the marked trails. Hills tend to be long but not particularly steep. This area lies within the snowbelt and holds snow well into spring.

Red Trail:

Trail	Distance
Red 1	1.6 miles
Red 2	0.8 mile
Red 3	0.2 mile connector
Red 4	0.3 mile
Red 5	0.5 mile

Bare Swamp State Forest continued:

Trail	Distance
Red 6	0.5 mile
R1, R6	2.1 mile loop
R1, R2, R4,R5	3.2 mile loop

Blue Trail:

Trail	Distance
Blue 1	0.7 mile
Blue 2	0.8 mile
Blue 3	0.5 mile
Blue 4	0.2 mile
Blue 5	0.2 mile dead end to overlook Bear Swamp
Blue 6	0.4 mile
Blue 7	0.6 mile
B1, B2, Y4, B3, B4, B6, B7	3.4 mile loop

Yellow Trail:

Trail	Distance
Yellow 1	1.1 mile loop
Yellow 2	0.8 mile
Yellow 3	0.6 mile
Yellow 4	0.2 mile
Yellow 5	0.3 mile
Yellow 6	1.7 miles
Yellow 7	0.2 mile
Yellow 8	0.2 mile
Yellow 9	0.9 mile
Y6, Y9, Y8	2.8 mile loop
Y2, Y3, Y4, Y5, Y9, Y8, Y7	3.2 mile loop

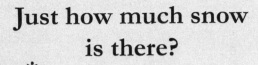

Just how much snow is there?

Western New York is known for its snowfall—it's all we talk about in winter. But, do we really get a lot of snow? The answer is yes and no. First of all, snow is very difficult to measure accurately because it settles, melts, and is blown into drifts by the winds. A search of records and statistics turns up a dizzying array of conflicting numbers.

The record for annual snowfall is now held by Mount Baker in the state of Washington which had a verified 1,140 inches of snow in the 1998-99 season. Western New York pales in comparison:

Buffalo	199 inches in 1976-77
Syracuse	192 inches in 1992-93
Rochester	112 inches in 1998-99

In an average year Western New York gets 90 to 110 inches of snow—a truly respectable amount.

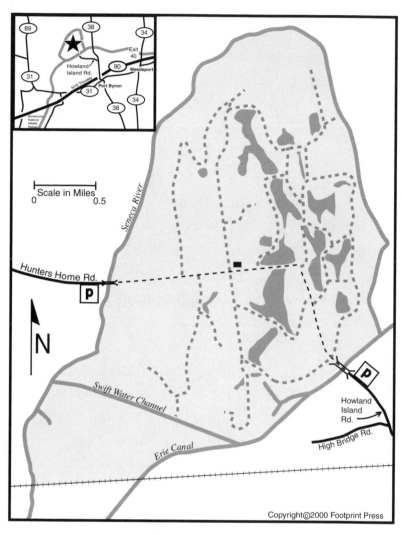

Howland Island

61.

Howland Island

Location:	Northwest of Port Byron, Cayuga County
Directions:	From Port Byron (between exits 40 & 41 on the NYS Thruway), head north on Route 38. Turn west on Howland Island Road and follow it to the closed bridge. Park along the right side of the road before the bridge.
Length:	19.5 miles of trails
Difficulty:	Intermediate
Terrain:	Western portion of island is flat, eastern is hilly
Trail Markings:	None
Uses:	Skiing, Snowshoeing, Hiking
Amenities:	None
Admission:	Free
Dogs:	OK
Hours:	Dawn to dusk
Contacts:	Howland Island Wildlife Area
	NYS Department of Environmental Conservation
	1285 Fisher Avenue, Cortland, NY 13045
	(607) 753-3095
	6274 E. Avon-Lima Road, Avon, NY 14414
	(716) 226-2466
	http://www.dec.state.ny.us
	Montezuma Wetlands Complex
	1385 Morgan Road, Savannah, NY 13146
	(315) 365-2371

For Snow Conditions Call: None

Waters of the Seneca River and the Erie Canal surround the 3,100 acres of Howland Island. The land was first settled and cleared for farming in the 1800s. Farming continued until the 1920s. The land was purchased as a game refuge in 1932 and became a Civilian Conservation Corps camp between 1933 and 1941. The CCC built 18 earthen dikes to create about 300 acres of water impoundments.

The rolling hills and steep drumlins above these impoundments are now home to a second growth mixture of hardwoods such as maple, ash, willow, basswood, black locust, oak, and hickory. The trails are abandoned gravel roads and old service vehicle tracks, now sufficiently overgrown to make pleasant trails.

If you encounter signs saying "Baited Area, hunting or entry within posted area prohibited," you can ignore them. DEC personnel clarified that hunting is prohibited in these areas, but recreational access is allowed.

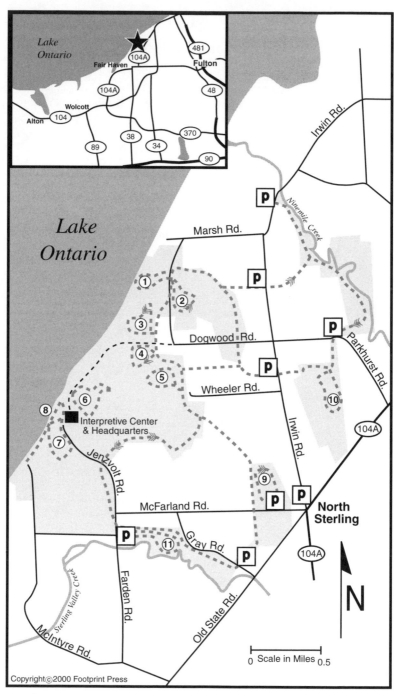

Sterling Lakeshore Park & Nature Center

62.

Sterling Lakeshore Park & Nature Center

Location:	North Sterling, Cayuga County
Directions:	Sterling Lakeshore Park is off Route 104A, between Fair Haven and Oswego. From Route 104A head north on Irwin Road for the ski trail parking area or west on McFarland Road, then north on Jenzvolt Road for the interpretive center.
Length:	16 miles of trails
Difficulty:	Novice, Intermediate
Terrain:	Steep drumlin hills & gently rolling hills
Trail Markings:	None (arrows & blazes planned for the future)
Uses:	Skiing, Snowshoeing, Hiking
Amenities:	Warming hut (interpretive center)
	Restrooms (interpretive center)
Admission:	Free (donation appreciated)
Dogs:	OK
Hours:	Dawn to dusk
Contact:	Sterling Nature Center
	PO Box 216, Sterling, NY 13156
	(315) 947-6143
	www.cayuganet.org/sterlingpark/

For Snow Conditions Call: (315) 947-6143

This spectacular 1,400-acre site, with nearly two miles of Lake Ontario shoreline, features glacially sculpted bluffs with scenic vistas of Lake Ontario. The land consists of a series of drumlins with intervening lowlands. The trails wind through a varied terrain of wetlands, vernal ponds, woodland, creeks, and meadows. This is a fairly new park and as such is a work in progress. They offer beginning level ski lessons in winter so call for the schedule.

Trail	Distance	Level of Difficulty
1, 2, 3, & 5	0.7 mile each	Intermediate
4, 6	0.7 mile each	Novice
7	0.6 mile	Novice
8, 9, 10, 11	0.5 mile each	Novice
Perimeter loops	9.5 miles	Intermediate

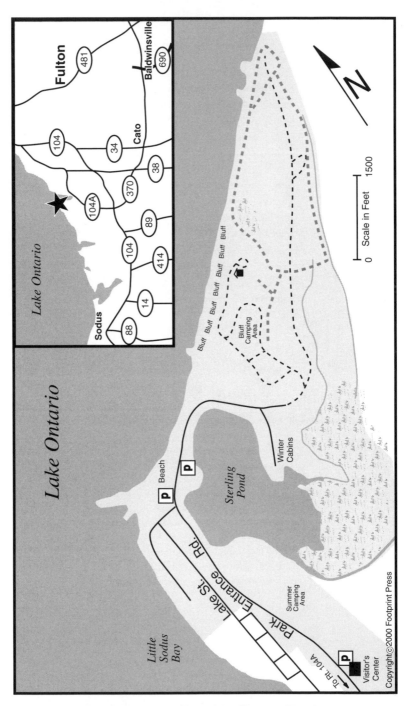

Fair Haven Beach State Park

63.

Fair Haven Beach State Park

Location:	Fair Haven, Cayuga County
Directions:	Take Route 104A west from Oswego or north from Route 104 to find Fair Haven Beach State Park.
Length:	3 miles of trails & unplowed roads
Difficulty:	Novice, Intermediate
Terrain:	Mild hills
Trail Markings:	None
Uses:	Skiing, Snowshoeing, Hiking
Amenities:	Restrooms
	Winter cabins available to rent
Admission:	Free ($6/car May-October)
Dogs:	OK on leash
Hours:	Dawn to dusk
Contact:	Fair Haven Beach State Park
	Route 104A, PO Box 16, Fair Haven, NY 13064
	(315) 947-5205

For Snow Conditions Call: (315) 947-5205

Perched on the shore of Lake Ontario, this park is busier in summer than winter. This is drumlin country so expect some hills. Bring your ice skates for a glide on Sterling Pond and watch the shore line for ice caves, chimney blow-holes and ice bridges. Other than the pond, stay solidly on ground, the ice banks can be extremely treacherous. The lake is a beautiful but dangerous place in winter.

What is lake-effect?

Two inland seas frame western and central New York. Lake Erie to the west and Lake Ontario to the north. Lake-effect storms occur when cold air blows over the warmer lake water. The air pulls moisture from the lakes. The moisture condenses, freezes, and falls and we're blanketed in blinding white stuff.

In the 1990s meteorologists used new doppler radar technology to track snowfall, wind speed, water temperature, and air temperature during lake-effect storms. They found temperature to be the major determinate of lake-effect storms. Snow is most likely when the lake surface temperature is 23 degrees warmer than the air at altitudes of up to 5,000 feet.

Lake-effect storms pack the potential for depositing more than 3 feet of snow at a time. You might as well go out and play in it.

Onondaga
County

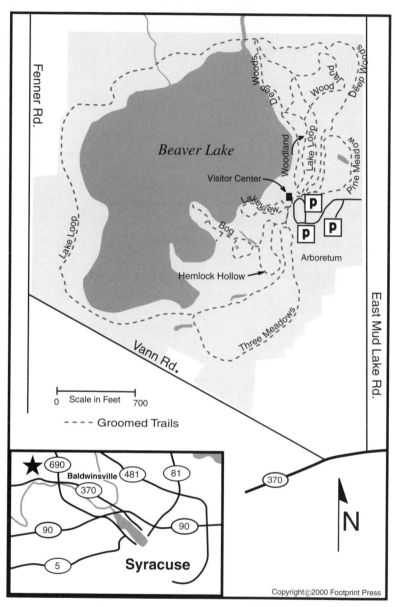

Beaver Lake Nature Center

64.

Beaver Lake Nature Center

Location:	Baldwinsville, Onondaga County
Directions:	From Route 370 (west off Route 690), turn north on East Mud Lake Road. The nature center entrance will be on the left.
Length:	9 miles of trails
Difficulty:	Novice
Terrain:	Mild hills
Trail Markings:	Black and white signs on posts
Uses:	Skiing, Snowshoeing, Hiking
Amenities:	Warming hut (nature center)
	Snack bar on weekends
	Snowshoe rentals ($1/hour)
	Restrooms
	Groomed trails
Admission:	$1 per vehicle
Dogs:	Pets NOT allowed
Hours:	7:30 AM to dusk
Contact:	Beaver Lake Nature Center
	8477 East Mud Lake Road, Baldwinsville, NY 13027
	www.co.onondaga.ny.us
	(315) 638-2519

For Snow Conditions Call: (315) 638-2519

Beaver Lake bustles in the winter with people enjoying the trails. The nature center offers classes in cross-country skiing, ice cutting, snowshoeing, and maple sugaring. The wide trails are well marked and easy-to-follow, perfect for a family outing.

Trail	Distance
Lakeview Trail	0.3 mile
Hemlock Hollow Trail	0.4 mile
Pine Meadow Trail	0.5 mile
Bog Trail	0.6 mile
Woodland Trail	1.1 miles
Deep Woods Trail	1.4 miles
Three Meadows Trail	1.5 miles
Lake Loop Trail	3.0 miles

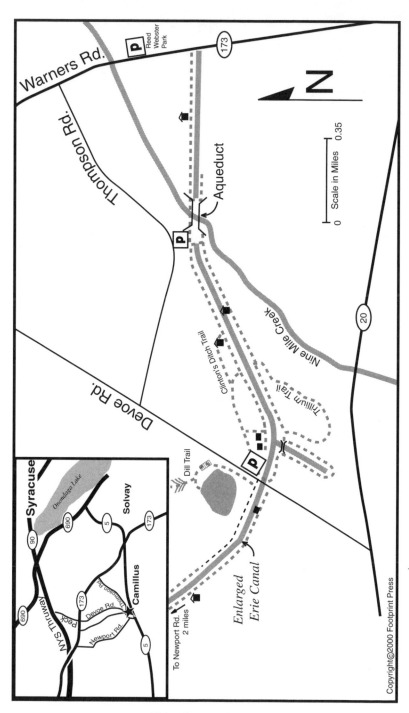

Erie Canal Park

65.

Erie Canal Park

Location:	Camillus, Onondaga County
Directions:	From Route 5, turn north on Devoe Road. Erie Canal Park is on the right, just south of Thompson Road.
Length:	10 miles of trails
Difficulty:	Novice
Terrain:	Flat
Trail Markings:	None
Uses:	Skiing, Snowshoeing, Hiking
Amenities:	Restroom in Sims' Store Shelters along the trail
Admission:	Free
Dogs:	OK on leash
Hours:	Dawn to dusk
Contacts:	Town of Camillus Erie Canal Park David Beebe, Director Sims' Museum 109 East Way, Camillus, NY 13031 (315) 488-3409
	Camillus Town Hall 4600 West Genesee Street, Syracuse, NY 13219 (315) 488-1234

For Snow Conditions Call: None

The enlarged Erie Canal was abandoned in 1922, then sat idle until 1972 when the town of Camillus purchased a seven-mile stretch. Since then an army of volunteers has been busy clearing the land, building dams, refilling the canal with water, and building a replica of Sims' store. The original Sims' store was built in 1856 at the intersection of Warners Road and the canal. It served as a general store, home for the Sims family, and departure point for people boarding the canal boats. The store was destroyed by fire in 1863, the replica lives on today. The first floor is setup like the original store. The second floor houses exhibits and antiques of the era along with models of locks, aqueducts, and canal boats. Sims' Museum is open Saturdays year-round from 9 AM - 1 PM, and Sundays from 1 PM - 5 PM, May through October, and 1 PM - 4 PM, November through April.

The trails circumnavigate the historic enlarged Erie Canal and parallel sections of the original Clinton's Ditch. They also take you over the aqueduct which carries the canal waters over Nine Mile Creek. Snowmobiles periodically use the towpath parallel to the canal but are not allowed on the side trails. The Dill Trail leads to Dill's Landing, which was once a wide waters and boat slip along Clinton's Ditch.

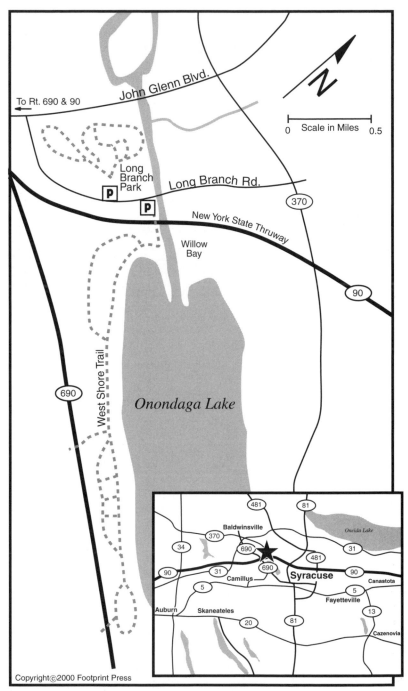

West Shore Trail & Long Branch Park

66.
West Shore Trail and Long Branch Park

Location:	Onondaga Lake shoreline, Liverpool, Onondaga County
Directions:	From I-90, take Liverpool exit 38. Head north on Route 57 (Oswego Road) then left (W) on Route 35 (Long Branch Road.) Cross the bridge over Onondaga Lake outlet then
park	on either side.
Length:	West Shore Trail - 3 mile loop
	Long Branch Park - 1.8 miles of loop trails
Difficulty:	Novice
Terrain:	Flat
Trail Markings:	None
Uses:	Skiing, Snowshoeing, Hiking
Amenities:	Restrooms at Willow Bay, porta-potty at Long Branch
Admission:	Free
Dogs:	OK on leash
Hours:	Dawn to dusk
Contact:	Onondaga Lake Park
	PO Box 146, Liverpool, NY 13088
	www.co.onondaga.ny.us
	(315) 453-6712

For Snow Conditions Call: (315) 453-6712

The trails on the east side of Onondaga Lake are a hive of activity in the summer but they're either plowed or wind blown in winter.

We recommend sticking to the western and northern sides. The West Shore Trail gets packed by snowmobilers in winter and the trees break the wind so it's a much more pleasant place to ski. There are plans to pave the main trail along Onondaga Lake but the tree canopy should help hold the snow. The trails heading south over I-690 are not skiable. They lead to housing developments.

The loops in Long Branch Park tend to hold snow well for an extended ski season. This area is used in warmer months by high school track teams.

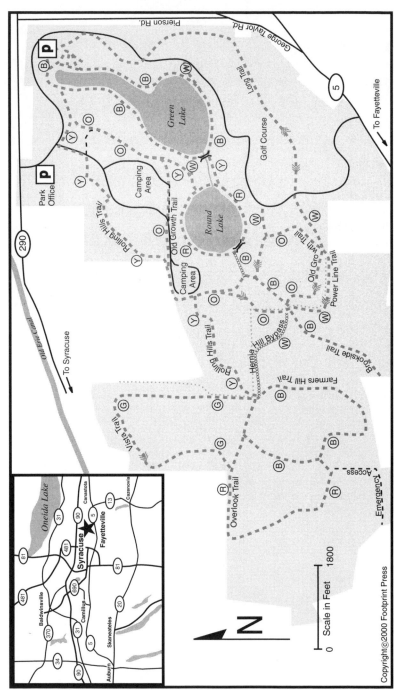

Green Lakes State Park

67.

Green Lakes State Park

Location:	Fayetteville, Onondaga County
Directions:	From I-690 in Syracuse, head east on Route 290 passing through East Syracuse. Watch for Green Lakes signs.
Length:	20 miles of trails
Difficulty:	Novice, Intermediate, Advanced
Terrain:	Rolling hills and open meadow
Trail Markings:	Colored blazes
Uses:	Skiing, Snowshoeing, Hiking
Amenities:	Restrooms (at park office, porta-potty at parking area)
Admission:	Free ($6/vehicle Memorial Day - Labor Day)
Dogs:	OK on leash (must clean up after your pet)
Hours:	Dawn to dusk
Contact:	Green Lakes State Park
	7900 Green Lakes Road, Fayetteville, NY 13066-9658
	www.nysparks.state.ny.us
	(315) 637-6111

For Snow Conditions Call: (315) 637-6111

Like Devil's Bathtub in Mendon Ponds Park south of Rochester, both Round and Green Lakes are meromictic lakes. Because they're set in deep circular basins, winds do not cause the mixing of surface water with bottom water. There is no seasonal turnover of the water as occurs with most lakes. The name meromictic derives from the mirrored effect of the still water. Originally thought by Indians and early travelers to be bottomless, Round Lake has been measured at 180 feet, while Green Lake is 195 feet deep. The shorelines of both lakes drop off quickly and deeply, making skiing or snowshoeing on the frozen water dangerous and illegal.

Round and Green Lakes are glacial lakes—products of the last ice age when an ice sheet more than 3,000 feet thick covered the area. About 10,000 years ago the ice sheet began to melt and recede northward. Torrents of water formed a glacial waterfall that carved the lake basins. The lakes are green. The color is due to a combination of factors—very deep, clear water, little suspended material or plant material in the water, and the presence of calcium carbonate. When light penetrates the water, the longer wavelengths (red end of the spectrum), are the first to be absorbed; only the blue and green wavelengths are transmitted to deeper water where they are reflected back to the observer.

There's a multitude of ski routes to choose from in this park. Visitors are encouraged to sign in at the trail register box located at the trailhead leading from the parking area. Use the following list to select a route consistent with your time available and skiing ability:

Green Lakes State Park continued:

Trail	Distance	Difficulty Level	Markings
Green Lake Trail	2.3 miles	Novice	Blue blazes
Round Lake Trail	0.8 mile	Novice	Red blazes

The lakes trails are wide and flat, passing through a forest of northern white cedar and hardwood trees. In winter, the green lakes contrast beautifully with the white snow.

Old Growth Trail	2.7 miles	Advanced	Orange blazes

This trail has steep sections and sharp turns but takes you through a forest of 200-year-old trees.

Power Line Trail	1.0 mile	Advanced	White blazes

For a good aerobic workout try this trail with its steep hills and gradual turns.

Long Trail	3.0 mile	Intermediate	Unblazed

An open trail though the golf course with spectacular views of Green Lake and the surrounding park. You'll find a challenging uphill climb and downhill adventure.

Brookside Trail	0.3 miles	Novice	Blue blazes

A flat trail through a dense forest, flanked by a small wetland.

Rolling Hills Trail	1.8 miles	Intermediate	Yellow blazes

This trail begins moderately difficult but eventually flattens out for a leisurely trip through a mixed conifer and hardwood forest.

Hernia Hill Bypass	0.2 mile	Advanced	White blazes

A steep trail for snowshoeing only.

Farmers Hill Trail	1.4 miles	Novice	Blue blazes

This open prairie-like trail is predominately flat with some small rolling hills.

Overlook Trail	1.1 miles	Novice	Red blazes

A flat trail with scenic overlooks of Fayetteville and its surroundings.

Vista Trail	1.4 miles	Intermediate	Green blazes

A diverse, hilly trail with views of Minoa Lakes and a deep ravine to ski at its northwestern leg.

Rick French of Pack, Paddle, Ski demonstrates telemark skiing.

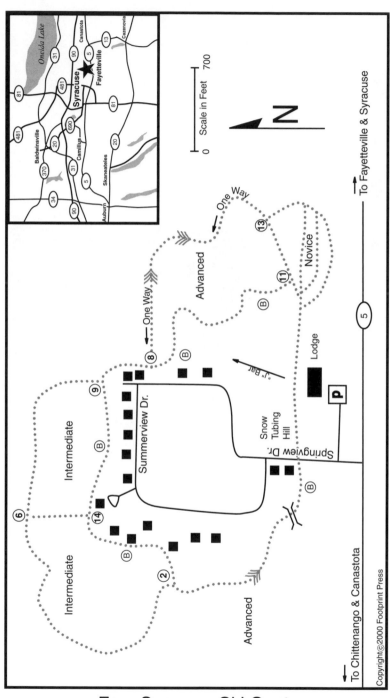

Four Seasons Ski Center

68.

Four Seasons Ski Center

Location:	Fayetteville, Onondaga County
Directions:	From Syracuse, head east on Route 5. Four Seasons is across from Green Lakes State Park.
Length:	6 miles of trails
Difficulty:	Novice, Intermediate, Advanced
Terrain:	Hilly
Trail Markings:	Junctions have red wooden signs with yellow numbers
Uses:	Skiing, Snowshoeing, Tubing
Amenities:	Warming hut
	Restrooms
	Snacks
	Rentals
	Groomed trails
Admission:	$4
Dogs:	Pets NOT allowed
Hours:	Monday-Tuesday 10 AM-5 PM
	Wednesday-Friday 10 AM-9:30 PM
	Saturday, Sunday, Holidays 10 AM-5 PM
Contact:	Four Seasons Golf & Ski Center
	8012 East Genesee Street, Fayetteville, NY 13066
	www.FourSeasonsGolfandSki.com
	(315) 637-9023

For Snow Conditions Call: (315) 637-9023

Four Seasons is a year-round recreation center. The winter activities include downhill skiing, cross-country skiing, snowshoeing, and tubing. In the summer bring your clubs for a golf practice range and miniature golf course.

The lodge is set in a valley at the base of a 100-foot downhill ski run. The cross-country areas include a flat, novice training area with set-tracks, and trails through the woods to scenic vistas. The trails head uphill circling the downhill skiing area and a grouping of homes.

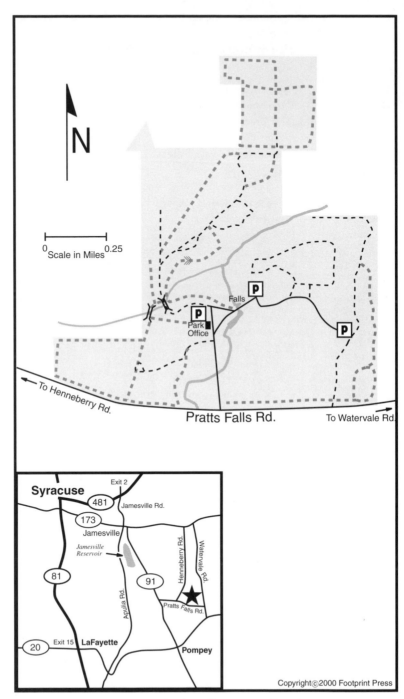

Pratt's Falls County Park

69.

Pratt's Falls County Park

Location:	Manlius, Onondaga County
Directions:	From Route 91, southeast of Syracuse, head east on Pratt's Falls Road.
Length:	9 miles of trails
Difficulty:	Novice, Intermediate, Advanced
Terrain:	Hilly
Trail Markings:	Round metal skier markers, blazes on trees, universal ski trail markers
Uses:	Skiing, Snowshoeing, Hiking
Amenities:	Wood stove and picnic table in park office
	Restrooms in park office
Admission:	$1 per vehicle
Dogs:	OK on leash
Hours:	6 AM to dusk
Contact:	Onondaga County Department of Parks
	Pratt's Falls Park
	7671 Pratt's Falls Road, Manlius, NY 13104
	www.co.onondaga.ny.us
	(315) 682-5934

For Snow Conditions Call: (315) 682-5934

Head to Pratt's Falls for peace and solitude. It gets little use in winter but offers scenic trails through pine forests, fields, and a stream gorge. We were impressed with the natural beauty of this park.

You'll see evidence of Civilian Conservation Corps work throughout the park in stone walls, buildings, and bridges. Pratt's Falls is a 137-foot falls that sometimes freezes over in winter. Ski into the gorge to view the falls and see if you can spot the rainbow which can be spectacular in winter against an all-white background when the mist in the air and the sunlight are at the right angle. This area was an early Indian camping ground and home to a sawmill, then grist mill in the late 1700s.

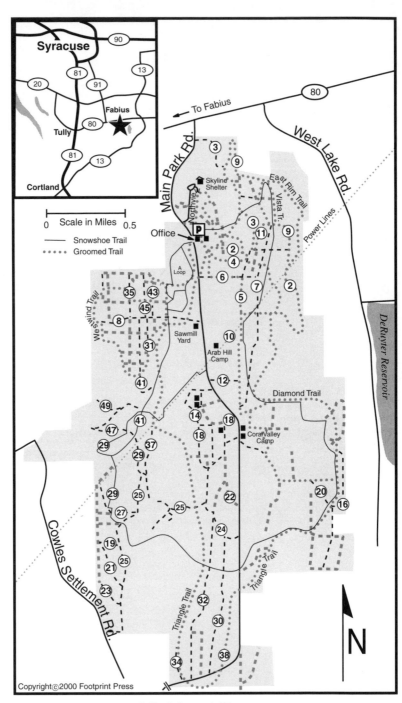

Highland Forest

70.

Highland Forest

Location:	Fabius, Onondaga County
Directions:	Exit I-81 at Tully (exit 14) and head east for 11 miles on Route 80. Turn left onto Main Park Road.
Length:	20 miles of trails
Difficulty:	Novice, Intermediate, Advanced
Terrain:	Varied
Trail Markings:	Ski trails are marked by a letter designating the trail name. Hiking/snowshoe trails have yellow pine tree symbol. Jeep and truck trails are numbered.
Uses:	Skiing, Snowshoeing, Hiking
Amenities:	Warming hut (rustic community house)
	Snack bar (weekends only)
	Vending machine room
	Ski trails are track-set groomed
	Horse drawn hay/sleigh rides
	Ski ($12/day) and snowshoe ($1/hour) rentals
Admission:	$1/vehicle
Dogs:	OK on leash on hike/snowshoe trails only
Hours:	Dawn to 4 PM
Contact:	Highland Forest
	PO Box 31, Highland Park Road, Fabius, NY 13063
	(315) 683-5550
	www.co.onondaga.ny.us

For Snow Conditions Call: (315) 683-5550

Highland Forest County Park comes alive in winter with the sounds of people having fun. In addition to 20 miles of ski trails which are monitored by a volunteer Nordic Ski Patrol, there's Skyline Hill for sledding, horse-drawn sleigh rides on weekends and holidays, and even a pioneer museum which transports you back to the 19th century, when settlers skied for survival.

The park is a network of trails, fire lanes, and truck trails that sits in a high land area, with Arab Hill being the high point (1,940 feet).

All ski trails start behind the park office. Stop in to pick up a larger, color map of the trail network. On weekends, all trails must be skied in a clockwise direction.

Note: because of the density of trails on this map, the hike/snowshoe trail is designated as a thin, solid line, not a series of xxx's as on other maps in this book.

See page 202 for a detailed trail listing.

Highland Forest continued:

Ski Trails	Distance	Marking	Level of Difficulty
North Run:			
Short & Sweet Trail	0.5 mile	S	Intermediate
Northview Trail	1.1 miles	N	Intermediate
West Run:			
Westwind Trail	3.0 miles	W	Novice
Westwind to Triangle trail	1.2 miles	W & T	Novice
South Run:			
Rectangle Trail	1.5 miles	Rectangle	Intermediate
Hexagon Short-cut Trail	3.0 miles	Hexagon	Intermediate
Diamond Trail	4.9 miles	Diamond	Intermediate
Triangle Trail	7.8 miles	Triangle	Intermediate
East Run:			
East Rim	2.5 miles	E	Advanced
Kamikaze Hill & East Rim	2.5 miles	K & E	Advanced
Vista Trail	1.8 miles	V	Advanced

Snowshoe Trails	Distance	Marking	Level of Difficulty
A Loop	0.9 mile	Yellow tree symbol	Novice
B Loop	1.2 miles	Yellow tree symbol	Novice
C Loop	2.7 miles	Yellow tree symbol	Intermediate
Easy Street	0.5 mile	Yellow tree symbol	Novice
Goat Trail	0.3 mile	Yellow tree symbol	Advanced
Large Loop	8.2 miles	Yellow tree symbol	Intermediate

Cortland
& Broome
Counties

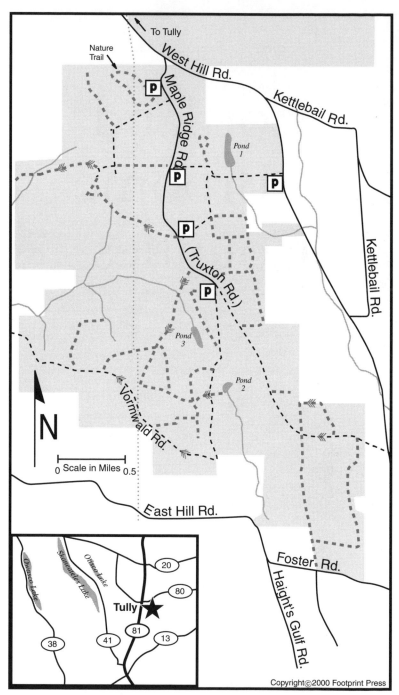

Heiberg Memorial Forest

71.

Heiberg Memorial Forest

Location: Tully, Cortland County

Directions: Exit I-81 at Tully and drive east on Route 80 for 1 mile. Turn right onto Railroad Street. At the end of the block, bear left and then right across the railroad tracks onto Grove Street. Grove Street becomes West Hill Road. Watch for the sign to Heiberg on your left. Turn right onto Maple Ridge Road (Truxton Road). Park in designated areas only.

Length: 12.6 miles of trails
8 miles of unplowed roads

Difficulty: Novice, Intermediate

Terrain: Rolling hills

Trail Markings: None

Uses: Skiing, Snowshoeing, Hiking

Amenities: None

Admission: Free

Dogs: OK on leash

Hours: Dawn to dusk

Contact: State University of New York College of Environmental Science & Forestry
1 Forestry Drive, Syracuse, NY 13210-2778
(315) 469-3053
www.esf.edu/

For Snow Conditions Call: None

Heiberg Memorial Forest is owned by the State University of New York College of Environmental Science & Forestry and is used as an outdoor classroom and experimental station. They graciously allow us "non-students" to ski their land.

Their land is Truxton Hill, a rolling hill area of unplowed roads, fire lanes and trails. High elevation (2,020 feet) means the area catches snow coming off Lake Ontario which accumulates three to four feet deep.

Trail	Distance
Nature Trail	1.0 mile loop
Park where Maple Ridge Road plowing ends and make the largest possible loop using unplowed Vormwald Road and trails	4.2 mile loop

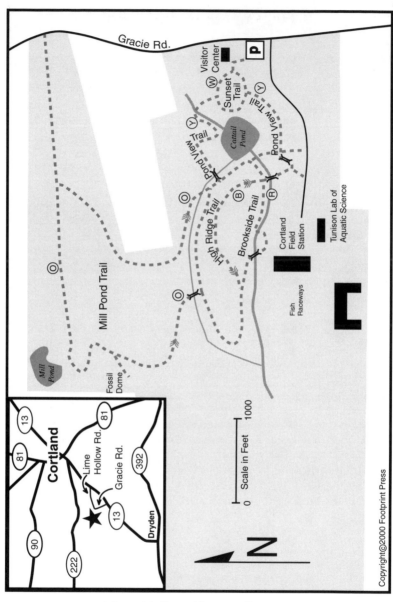

Lime Hollow Nature Center

72.

Lime Hollow Nature Center

Location:	Southwest of Cortland, Cortland County
Directions:	Follow Route 13 south from Cortland. Turn north on Gracie Road. Parking will be on the west side of Gracie Road at the sign "Tunison Lab of Aquatic Science."
Length:	4 miles of trails
Difficulty:	Novice, Intermediate
Terrain:	Hilly
Trail Markings:	Color-coded, geometric-shaped trail markers on posts
Uses:	Skiing, Snowshoeing, Hiking
Amenities:	Warming hut (nature center)
	Restrooms (in nature center)
Admission:	Free
Dogs:	OK on leash
Hours:	Dawn to dusk
Contact:	Lime Hollow Nature Center
	3091 Gracie Road, Cortland, NY 13045-9355
	(607) 758-5462

For Snow Conditions Call: (607) 758-5462

Lime Hollow Nature Center covers 115 acres of diverse woodlands with five loop trails available for winter enjoyment. There is a visitor center with interpretive exhibits and live animal exhibits. The visitor center is open Monday through Saturday from 9 AM to 4 PM and Sunday from 1 PM to 4 PM.

A unique feature of Lime Hollow is the Tunison Lab of Aquatic Science, which is open to visitors. Salmon, rainbow, and lake trout can be seen in indoor raceways.

The trails are well marked with signs coded by color and geometric shape:

Trail	Marking	Distance	Level of Difficulty
Sunset Trail	White diamonds	0.3 mile	Novice
Pondview Trail	Yellow circles	0.85 mile	Novice
Brookside Trail	Red triangle	1.0 mile	Novice
High Ridge Trail	Blue squares	0.25 mile	Intermediate
Mill Pond Trail	Orange hexagons	1.5 miles	Intermediate

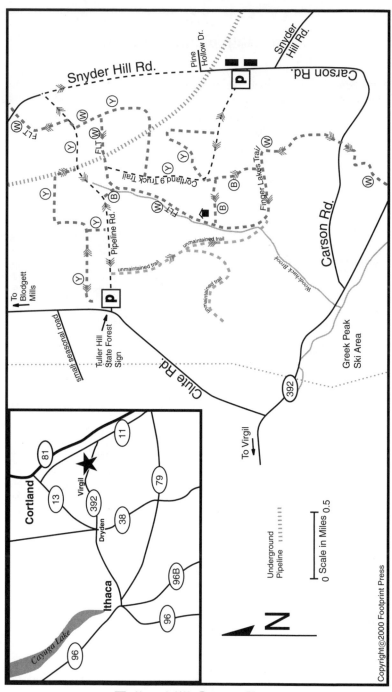

Tuller Hill State Forest

73.

Tuller Hill State Forest

Location:	Blodgett Mills, Cortland County
Directions:	From Route 392, east of Virgil and north of Greek Peak Ski Area, turn north on Clute Road. Park at top of hill near unplowed Pipeline Road. Or, from Route 392, head east on Carson Road, then north on Snyder Hill Road until the plowing ends.
Length:	9 miles of trails and unplowed roads
Difficulty:	Intermediate, Advanced
Terrain:	Hilly
Trail Markings:	Finger Lakes Trail is blazed white, side trails are blazed blue, other sections have round, yellow markers
Uses:	Skiing, Snowshoeing, Hiking
Amenities:	Shelter with outhouse
Admission:	Free
Dogs:	OK on leash
Hours:	Dawn to dusk
Contacts:	NYS Department of Environmental Conservation
	1285 Fisher Avenue, Cortland, NY 13045
	(607) 753-3095
	www.dec.state.ny.us
	Finger Lakes Trail Conference
	PO Box 18048, Rochester, NY 14618-0048
	(716) 288-7191
	www.fingerlakes.net/trailsystem

For Snow Conditions Call: None

This is an area of variety with peaked hilltops, rounded knolls, deep ravines, and gentle slopes. The trails and unplowed dirt roads wander through hardwood forests and tight stands of evergreens. Follow the unplowed roads for intermediate level skiing and the trails (such as Finger Lakes Trail) for an advanced adventure. Be aware that the map shows marked ski trails. Other snowmobile and illegal ATV trails do cross through the area.

Due to its high elevation, the snow accumulates deep here and lasts under the woods' shade.

Trail	Distance
Pipeline Road (Clute Rd. parking lot to Snyder Hill Rd.)	1.6 miles
FLT between Snyder Hill Rd & Carson Road	3.5 miles
Cortland Nine Truck Trail (from Carson Rd. parking area to FLT intersection near Pipeline Rd.)	1.7 miles

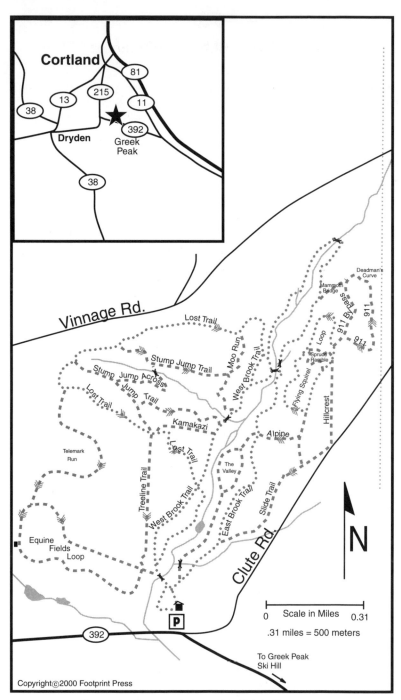

Greek Peak Nordic Ski Center

74.

Greek Peak Nordic Ski Center

Location:	Virgil, Cortland County
Directions:	From I-81 take exit 10 and head south on Route 215. Turn east on Route 392. The Touring Center is on the left (a small brown building) before Greek Peak Ski Resort.
Length:	10 miles of trails
Difficulty:	Novice, Intermediate, Advanced
Terrain:	Hilly
Trail Markings:	Ski signs (green dot = beginners, blue square = intermediate, black diamond = advanced, skull & crossbones = expert)
Uses:	Skiing, Snowshoeing
Amenities:	Warming hut, restrooms, snacks
	Groomed trails
	Ski ($12/day) and snowshoe ($10/day) rentals
	Lessons available
Admission:	$8 trail pass
Dogs:	Pets NOT Allowed
Hours:	Monday - Friday, 10 AM - 5 PM
	Saturday & Sunday, 9 AM - sunset
Contact:	Greek Peak Ski Resort
	2000 NYS Route 392, Cortland, NY 13045-9541
	(607) 835-6111
	www.greekpeak.net

For Snow Conditions Call: 1-800-365-SNOW

The Greek Peak Nordic Ski Center is separate from Greek Peak (downhill) Ski Resort and is located kitty-corner across Route 392. A multi-year plan calls for development of a golf course on this land, so the trails will be changing each year. Pick up a current map when you pay admission.

Both private and group ski lessons are available.

Trail	Distance	Level of Difficulty
West Brook	1.1 miles	Novice/Intermediate
East Brook	1.1 miles	Novice/Intermediate
The Valley	0.8 mile	Novice/Intermediate
Alpine	0.2 mile	Intermediate
Hillcrest	0.3 mile	Intermediate
Slide	0.3 mile	Intermediate
Lost Trail	1.1 miles	Advanced
Treeline	0.3 mile	Advanced
Kamakazi	0.2 mile	Advanced

Greek Peak Nordic Ski Center continued:

Trail	Distance	Level of Difficulty
Stump Jump	1.3 miles	Advanced
Moo Run	0.1 mile	Intermediate
Jump Across	0.3 mile	Advanced
Mamouth Bridge	0.1 mile	Intermediate
911	0.4 mile	Advanced
911 Bypass	0.2 mile	Intermediate
Flying Squirrel Loop	0.7 mile	Intermediate
Spruce Ramble	0.1 mile	Intermediate
Telemark Run	0.6 mile	Intermediate
Equine Fields Loop	1.0 mile	Intermediate

 To prevent frostbite and hypothermia, pay special attention to protecting your feet, hands, face, and top of head. Up to 40% of body heat can be lost when the head is exposed. Dress in layers so you can remove a layer to avoid perspiration.

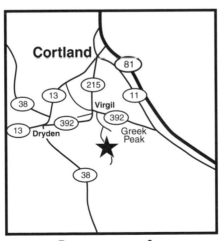

Locator map for
James B. Kennedy State Forest

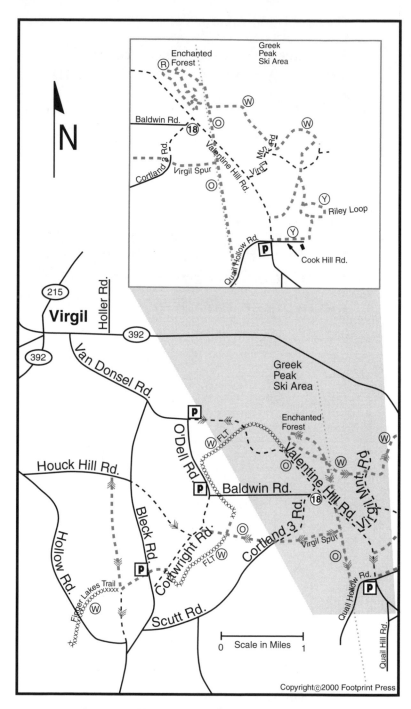

James B. Kennedy State Forest

75.

James B. Kennedy State Forest

Location:	Virgil, Cortland County
Directions:	From Route 392 in Virgil, turn south onto VanDonsel Road. Park where the plowing ends. Or, continue east on 392, turn south on Parker Street Road (county route 132) in East Virgil. Then turn north on Valentine Hill Road and park when the plowing ends. (See locator map on page 213.)
Length:	15 miles of trails and unplowed roads
Difficulty:	Intermediate, Advanced
Terrain:	Hilly
Trail Markings:	Finger Lakes Trail is white blazed, The Virgil Spur of FLT is orange blazed, unplowed Valentine Road is marked as snow mobile route 5A, Enchanted Forest is marked with red ply wood squares, other sections have round, yellow ski markers
Uses:	Skiing, Snowshoeing
Amenities:	None
Admission:	Free
Dogs:	OK on leash
Hours:	Dawn to dusk
Contacts:	NYS Department of Environmental Conservation 1285 Fisher Avenue, Cortland, NY 13045 (607) 753-3095 www.dec.state.ny.us Finger Lakes Trail Conference PO Box 18048, Rochester, NY 14618-0048 (716) 288-7191 www.fingerlakes.net/trailsystem

For Snow Conditions Call: None

About 8 miles south of Cortland, this high elevation area (approximately 2,000 feet) receives good snow. It includes Greek Peak (the back side of Greek Peak Ski Resort) and Virgil Mountain with a series of trails and unplowed roads. Most hills are moderate steepness but there are some steep sections.

Trail	Distance	Level of Difficulty
Unplowed Valentine Hill Road	3.5 miles	Intermediate
Virgil Spur	2.0 miles	Advanced

Loop from Cook Hill Road,
  through Riley Loop and Enchanted Forest,
  returning by Valentine Hill Road
	7.0 miles	Advanced

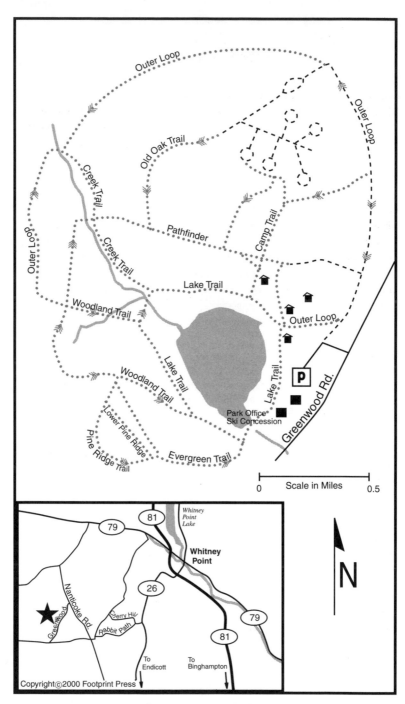

Greenwood Park

76.

Greenwood Park

Location:	Nanticoke, Broome County
Directions:	From Route 81, it's 10.5 miles to the park. Take Route 26 south. In 4.5 miles, turn west on Cherry Hill Road, then bear left on Rabbit Path Road. At the end turn left then a quick right on Henry M. Baldwin Street. At the T, turn right on Nanticoke Road. Turn left onto Greenwood Road. Greenwood Park will be on the right in 1 mile.
Length:	5.5 miles of trails
Difficulty:	Novice, Intermediate, Advanced
Terrain:	Hilly
Trail Markings:	Some trail names on brown posts at intersections
Uses:	Skiing, Snowshoeing, Hiking
Amenities:	Shelter
	Groomed trails
	Ski Rentals ($2.50/hour)
Admission:	$3/day, $20 season pass
Dogs:	Pets NOT allowed
Hours:	8 AM - 4 PM weekdays, 9 AM - 4 PM weekends
Contact:	Broome County Department of Parks & Recreation
	PO Box 1766, Binghampton, NY 13902
	(607) 862-9933

For Snow Conditions Call: None

Greenwood Park sports a man-made pond nestled in a valley below surrounding hills. The trails are wide, gently sloping swaths through a mature forest. Unplowed roads add to the network of trails in winter.

Trail	Distance	Level of Difficulty
Outer Loop	1.5 miles	Advanced
Lake Loop	1.0 mile	Novice
Evergreen	0.4 mile	Advanced
Lower Pine Ridge	0.2 mile	Advanced
Pine Ridge	0.5 mile	Advanced
Woodland	0.6 mile	Novice
Creek	0.5 mile	Novice
Pathfinder	0.4 mile	Novice
Old Oak	0.5 mile	Novice
Camp Trail	0.1 mile	Advanced

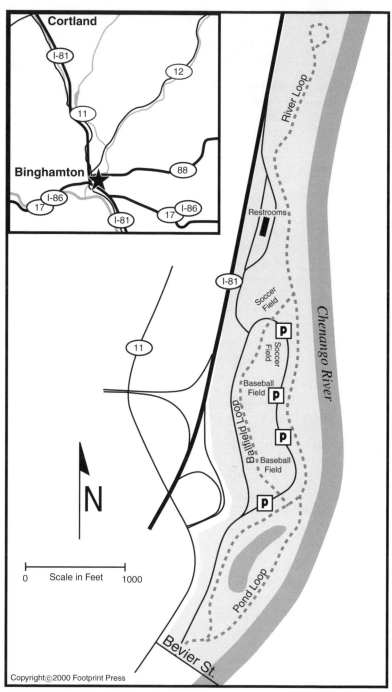

Otsiningo Park

77.

Otsiningo Park

Location:	Binghampton, Broome County
Directions:	From Route 17 (now I-86) exit onto Route 11 north. Turn right on Bevier Street and left into Otsiningo Park.
Length:	2.7 miles of trails
Difficulty:	Novice
Terrain:	Flat
Trail Markings:	None
Uses:	Skiing, Snowshoeing, Hiking
Amenities:	Restroom
Admission:	Free
Dogs:	OK on leash
Hours:	Dawn to dusk
Contact:	Broome County Department of Parks & Recreation PO Box 1766, Binghampton, NY 13902 (607) 778-2193

For Snow Conditions Call: None

Paved paths loop through this park of widely spaced trees and mowed grass areas. Winter, when leaves are off the trees, affords the best views of the Chenango River.

Trail	Distance	Level of Difficulty
River Loop (round trip)	1.1 miles	Novice
Ballfield Loop	0.9 mile	Novice
Pond Loop	0.7 mile	Novice

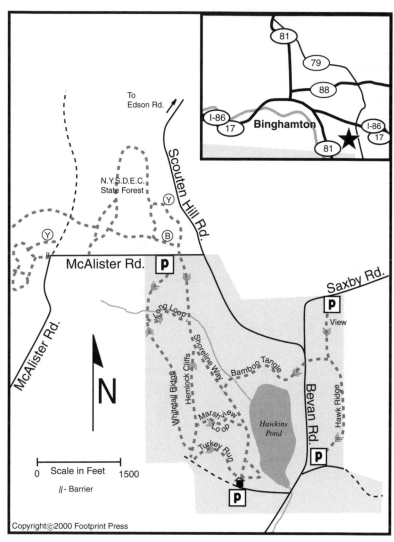

Hawkins Pond Nature Area

78.

Hawkins Pond Nature Area

Location:	Windsor, Broome County
Directions:	8 miles from Route 17 (I-86). Exit I-86 at Windsor (exit 79) and head south on Route 79. In South Windsor turn west on Edson Road then south on Scouten Hill Road. Bear right on Bevan Road. The nature area entrance will be on the right.
Length:	8 miles of trails
Difficulty:	Novice, Intermediate, Advanced
Terrain:	Hillside
Trail Markings:	Nature area has grey wooden posts with trail names at trail junctions
	DEC land has 2-inch round, yellow plastic markers
Uses:	Skiing, Snowshoeing, Hiking
Amenities:	Shelter
	Restrooms in shelter
Admission:	Free
Dogs:	OK on leash
Hours:	8 AM to dusk
Contact:	Broome County Department of Parks & Recreation
	PO Box 1766, Binghampton, NY 13902
	(607) 693-1389

For Snow Conditions Call: None

You'll be heading downhill as you drive Scouten Hill and Bevan Road to the base of a large pond. This means that the ski trails generally head uphill from the main parking area on Bevan Road. But, the trails are 6-feet wide and nicely graded, making for easy skiing. Most of the trails run through a young forest and shrub lands. Hawk Run has the steepest incline, through grasslands to a scenic overlook.

The DEC trails north of McAlister Road are narrower and less well maintained but are great for winter solitude.

Trail	Distance	Marking	Level of Difficulty
Hawk Ridge	0.6 mile	Trail name post	Advanced
Bamboo Tangle	0.4 mile	Trail name post	Novice
Shoreline Way	0.8 mile	Trail name post	Novice
Marshview Loop	0.2 mile	Trail name post	Intermediate
Turkey Run	0.2 mile	Trail name post	Novice
Hemlock Cliffs	0.4 mile	Trail name post	Intermediate
Whitetail Ridge	0.8 mile	Trail name post	Advanced
Long Loop	0.2 mile	Trail name post	Novice
DEC Trails	4.0 miles	Yellow markers	Intermediate

Definitions

Aqueduct:
A stone, wood, or cement trough built to carry waters over an existing creek or river. The world's largest aqueduct for its time was built in Rochester to carry the Erie Canal over the Genesee River. Eleven stone arches were erected, spanning 804 feet, to withstand the annual floods of this wild river.

Blaze:
A rectangular swath of paint used on trees to mark the path of a trail.

CCC:
Civilian Conservation Corps

DEC:
Department of Environmental Conservation

Doppler Radar:
Radar that uses the Doppler effect to measure velocity of storm fronts. Doppler effect is an apparent change in the frequency of waves occurring when the source and observer are in motion relative to each other.

Drumlin:
An elongated or oval hill created from glacial debris.

Esker:
A ridge of debris formed when a river flowed under the glacier in an icy tunnel. Rocky material accumulated on the tunnel beds, and when the glacier melted, a ridge of rubble remained.

FLT:
Finger Lakes Trail: a 500-mile long trail across New York State.

Gorp:
An abbreviation for "good old raisins and peanuts." It is used today to cover any combination of snacks taken to eat while enjoying outdoors activities.

Kames
Hills formed by rivers that flowed on top of the glacier and spilled over the edge depositing soil into huge piles.

Kettles
A pond created when a large block of ice separated from the glacier. Water running off of the glacier deposited gravel and debris all around the ice block. The block melted, leaving behind a rough circular depression.

Meromictic lake:
A very deep body of water surrounded by high ridges. Because the high ridges prevent the wind from blowing on the water, a motionless surface gives the lake a mirrored effect.

Sitzmark:
A hollow made in the snow by a skier who has fallen.

Swamp:
Wet, spongy land saturated and sometimes partially or inter-mittently covered with water.

Switchbacks:
Winding the trail back and forth across the face of a steep area to make the incline more gradual.

Telemark Skiing: Skiing downhill on cross-country skis, using turns in which the knees are bent, the inside heel is lifted, and the weight is on the outside ski, which is advanced ahead of the other and angled inward until the turn is complete.

Topographic map: Maps showing elevation through the use of contour lines.

Trestle:
A framework consisting of vertical, slanted supports and horizontal crosspieces supporting a bridge. This construction is often used for railroad bridges.

Vernal Pond:
A pond which is only filled with water in the spring.

Groomed Trails

High Elevation Trails

Ski Rentals Available

Snowshoe Rentals Available

Novices Start Here

Fun for the More Advanced

Scenic Trails

Spend All Day (over 20 miles of trails)

PUT YOURSELF INTO THE WINTER PICTURE!

WE PROVIDE ADVENTURE AND INSTRUCTION HERE OR THROUGHOUT THE WORLD!

From cold and snow to sun and surf or other adventure activities in between.

Contact Fellow Adventurous Spirits At:

PACK, PADDLE, SKI
BOX 82, S. LIMA, NY 14558

(716) 346-5597
Email: info@PackPaddleSki.com
Web: www.PackPaddleSki.com

Word Index

Other Books Available From Footprint Press

Take a Hike! Family Walks in the Rochester (NY) Area
  ISBN# 0-9656974-79   U.S. $16.95
  A guide to 60 trails for day hikes in Monroe County. Each trail has a
  map, description, and details you'll need such as where to park, estimated hiking time, and interesting points along the way.

Take Your Bike! Family Rides in the Rochester (NY) Area
  ISBN# 0-9656974-28   U.S. $16.95
  Converted railroad beds, paved bike paths, woods trails, and little used
  country roads combine to create the 30 safe bicycle adventures within
  an easy drive of Rochester, N.Y. No need to have a mountain bike –
  any sturdy bicycle will do.

Take A Hike! Family Walks in the Finger Lakes & Genesee Valley Region (NY)
  ISBN# 0-9656974-95   U.S. $16.95
  Perfect for an afternoon walk, ramble, or hike on 51 trails through
  forests, glens, and bogs of upstate N.Y. Each trail has a map, description, and details you'll need such as where to park, estimated hiking
  time, and interesting points along the way.

Take Your Bike! Family Rides in the Finger Lakes & Genesee Valley Region (NY)
  ISBN# 0-9656974-44   U.S. $16.95
  Converted railroad beds, paved bike paths, woods trails, and little used
  country roads combine to create the 40 safe bicycle adventures through
  central and western N.Y. No need to have a mountain bike – any
  sturdy bicycle will do.

Bruce Trail – An Adventure Along the Niagara Escarpment
  ISBN# 0-9656974-36   U.S. $16.95
  Join experienced backpackers on a five-week journey along the Niagara
  Escarpment in Ontario, Canada. Explore the now abandoned Welland
  Canal routes, caves formed by crashing waves, ancient cedar forests,
  and white cobblestone beaches along azure Georgian Bay. Learn the
  secrets of long-distance backpackers. As an armchair traveler or in
  preparation for a hike of your own, enjoy this ramble along a truly
  unique part of North America.

Peak Experiences – Hiking the Highest Summits of New York, County by County
  ISBN# 0-9656974-01   U.S. $16.95
  Bag the highest point in each of the 62 counties of New York State
  with this guidebook. Some are barely molehills that can be driven by,
  others are significant mountain peaks that require a full-day climb.
  All promise new discoveries.

Backpacking Trails of Central and Western NY
                         U.S. $2.00
  A 10-page booklet describing the backpackable trails of central and
  western New York State with contact information to obtain maps and
  trail guides.

For sample maps and chapters explore web site:
http://www.footprintpress.com

Yes, I'd like to order Footprint Press books:

#

____ *Snow Trails - Cross-country Ski in Central & Western NY*	$16.95
____ *Peak Experiences - Hiking the Summits of NY Counties*	$16.95
____ *Take A Hike! Family Walks in the Rochester (NY) Area*	$16.95
____ *Take A Hike! Family Walks in the Finger Lakes (NY)*	$16.95
____ *Take Your Bike! Family Rides in the Rochester (NY) Area*	$16.95
____ *Take Your Bike! Family Rides in the Finger Lakes (NY)*	$16.95
____ *Bruce Trail - Adventure Along the Niagara Escarpment (Canada)*	$16.95
____ *Backpacking Trails of Central & Western NY*	$2.00
____ *Alter – A Simple Path to Emotional Wellness*	$16.95

Sub-total $_____

NYS and Canadian residents add 8% tax $_____

Shipping is FREE $ FREE

Total enclosed: $_____

Your Name: _____

Address: _____

City: _____ State (Province): _____

Zip (Postal Code): _____ Country: _____

Make check payable and mail to:
Footprint Press
P.O. Box 645
Fishers, N.Y. 14453

**Or, check the web site at http://www.footprintpress.com
Or, call 1-800-431-1579**

Footprint Press books are available at special discounts
when purchased in bulk for sales promotions,
premiums, or fund raising.
Call (716) 421-9383 for details.